Enemies of the Cross

Javier Macias

Glorified Publishing
PO Box 8004
The Woodlands, TX 77387
www.GlorifiedPublishing.com

DEDICATION

This book is totally dedicated to the Body of Christ! True seekers of God the Father, which art in heaven. Hallowed be thy name! The one and only name given unto mankind for the Salvation of our souls! "Salvation is found in no one else Jesus, for there is no other name under heaven given to mankind by which we must be saved." (Acts 4:12)(NIV) Jesus Christ!

CONTENTS

ACKNOWLEDGMENTS

First and foremost I would like to acknowledge God, my Father for accepting me as his servant in doing his work through delivering messages for him unto his chosen people. I would also like to acknowledge my wife, Polly Macias along with my children Amanda, Samantha, Nikki, Thishalena, Javier Jr., Paulina and Rosalina who have all supported me in my calling of God in my personal life!

Chapter 1 - Thanksgiving 2015

"Sharpen the arrows, take up the shields! The Lord has stirred up the kings of the Medes, because his purpose is to destroy Babylon. The Lord will take vengeance, vengeance for his temple."   (Jeremiah 51:11 NIV)

Is there any human being on the face of this earth that has not contemplated revenge in some form as retaliation against someone who offended or hurt you? Probably not! Everybody wants to get even in a sense of obtaining justice of some kind in their painful experience.

But I say to my child: *"Do not take revenge, my dear friends, but leave room for God's wrath. For it is written: 'It's mine to avenge I will repay,' says the Lord."*   (Romans 12:19 NIV)

You will see in the coming days that I know exactly how *my people* feel. I AM about to take vengeance for "my temple" says the Spirit of God!

Vengeance for His temple? Yes, vengeance for "My temple"! While many are looking at what is going on all around them and what is happening, many come to the conclusion that *the Day of the Lord* is near. The anticipation of it has been around for several years now yet, Jesus Christ hasn't come **YET!**

God is not going to make it that easy for us to figure out when He comes. In fact, all of you know, whether you follow me or not, it is written, *"No one knows about that day or hour, not even the Angels in heaven,*

NOR THE SON, but only the Father."   *(Matthew 24:36 NIV)*

All He said was to watch for the signs that he spoke of to His disciples. Stand up! Your redemption draws nigh! *"When these things begin to take place, stand up and lift your heads, because your redemption draws near."*   *(Luke 21:28 NIV)*

Every sign he spoke of, apart from natural phenomenon, would involve occasions that could cause the death of many: nation rising against nation, kingdom against kingdom, famines, earthquakes in various places, and so on. It has been going on for years on end, yet He hasn't come! So the anticipation of his return has been taken to the grave by millions.

But for now, the message you get when He says stand up and lift your heads because your redemption draws near is pertaining to your personal life. In the case of being amidst all Jesus Christ spoke about before his return, your job is to give yourself over to Him with a sincere heart of repentance just in case you are a casualty of those end time events of which Jesus Christ spoke.

You are not going to change God's word that tears down, and destroys and builds up. He will tear you down, only to build you up in Himself. He will take YOU by whatever your name is, and tear that name down in your life for ONLY ONE reason: to exalt the name of the Lord Jesus Christ!

Your spirit and soul will be in God's eternal presence for your obedience to Jesus Christ's spoken word of standing up and lifting up your head unto the heavens of God your creator.

Much of what He spoke of has been going on right before our very eyes for many years and years without number, even years before any of us were born into this world we live in. We as a nation have been witnesses to catastrophic events that have unfolded before our very eyes which involved weather and other natural events over which we have no control.

We have also witnessed catastrophic evil and wicked events of murder right before our very eyes. In this great country of ours known as the United States of America, we witnessed just in recent years one of the greatest, evil acts of terrorism on our own soil: the September 11th attacks known as "911", not to mention the federal building in Oklahoma City, Oklahoma in 1995. Then we witness our own young children carry out execution style school shootings that have taken out many innocent children's lives in recent years. We have seen racial tensions over innocent lives being taken out in our very own society.

So, yes, we have had our share of nation against nation, kingdom against kingdom, not to mention earthquakes and famines. The problem with all this is: we take Jesus Christ's words at a minimum of what He said, and apply our own conclusion to His words. We see all the evil and atmospheric global weather activity all around us, and we anxiously await His return. We forget that he said that these are, "…*the beginning of birth pains."*   *(Matthew 24:8 NIV)*

Birth pains? Yes, as a woman gets when a new life is about to be birthed. Considering *the church,* the body of believers is called *the bride* in our Bibles, she is the woman I am giving this message to. Let me assure you that Jesus Christ's second coming is a highly debated topic within the the body of Christ itself. The debate is when he comes, what will be going on, and who goes through what, and who goes where, who endures prophetic events, and who doesn't.

I myself have personally experienced, and watched, while I listened to all this going on around me. Where I stand on my belief and my faith in that subject isn't really that important. Of course, as you read this message the Lord gave me, you will see my stance on that very subject. Rest assured, I only stand on that faith because of the messages the Lord has given me over the years that I have never shared with anyone, up until now.

And I sincerely ask that you take the time to go to God over what you are about to read in this book for your own good. You can believe what you want, and I will believe what I know the Lord has revealed to me. It's not a matter of who's right, and who's not. It's a matter of getting done what needs to be done before our Lord and Savior, Jesus Christ, comes. In the end, the truth be known! But in the meantime, begin a preparation for me, says the Lord. This is what I am being told to do. Preparation is not based on how you feel, or how I feel, or how you think, or how I think.

Let's use a true loving family as an example: Dad, Mom and the children. Do all of you think the same? No! Do all of you feel the same towards the issues of life and lifestyles? No! Do all of you like the same music? No! Do you like all the same foods, clothing styles, movies, books, etc.? No! We are all different. Yet you all love each other, right?

That is what I am trying to get you to understand before you go into this book you are reading. Sounds like I am trying to please everyone, and fit in. Well, I'm not! I have never been one to try and fit into anything, or anyone's mold of acceptance. Then what are you doing? I am trying to help you keep an open mind in reading this book, before Satan blinds you over anything you might get out of this book because of the way you feel, or think.

That was why I used the family example! Not a one of them feels or thinks the same, yet they live with one another. That was Jesus' greatest command: Love one another! Yet, despite His command and His heart-prayer of unity among His people, all I see are arguments and differences of all types among his so-called followers and believers. Total Division! It is totally opposite from Jesus Christ's heart's desire.

It makes me want to do more in my own personal effort of bringing more of Jesus Christ out of me in sharing Him more in this world than I already do, especially among my so-called brothers and sisters in Christ. Why? Because no matter when Jesus Christ comes, or how He comes, one thing is evident according to the word of God that does not lie, because it is written:

"For it is time for judgment to begin with God's household and if it begins with us, what will the outcome be for those who do not obey the gospel of God?"

(1 Peter 4:17 NIV)

So! It's imminent that a judgment is coming that will affect all believers, right? We are God's household! Or we should be! He is speaking of "the church", and it begins with us! Then it is asked, "If it begins with us, what will the outcome be to those **WHO DO NOT OBEY** the gospel of God?"

Can you see how God will do his final separating of the sheep from the goats, or the harvest from the weeds, and the good fish from the bad fish? Yet, there is a stirring of God in my spirit, even amidst such evil in this world we live in. I personally have spiritual encounters of love and mercy from God our Father in heaven. He shares with me His concern for His people.

Let me share this one particular moment in my life over God's love and concern for His people He loves so much. During the Thanksgiving holidays, of 2015, my wife and I decided to go visit my mother who lives three and a half hours away. During the visit, one of my nieces came over to visit us at my mother's house. Praise God, she is a born again believer who is on fire for Jesus Christ!

In our time of visitation, we discussed the lack of spiritual advancement within the kingdom of God here on the earth. It was not us doubting God, or His existence here on earth. It was more the failing of the church - the body of Christ - in receiving what is rightfully ours, courtesy of God our Father in heaven. It was given to us in order for it to be given to others.

I told my niece, "We have literally failed to capitalize on what Jesus

Christ has given to us for our own good, given for edifying the body of Christ." In the middle of our conversation, my niece asked me, "Do you think you can come this way once a month to teach what the Lord shares with you?"

I didn't answer her with a definite *yes*, or a definite *no*! All I said was, "I have to ask the Lord."

I never act on my own impulse, or my own thoughts in giving into circumstances that would involve my personal life in one way or another. As I taught my children, important life changing decisions should be brought before the Lord for His divine guidance in the right direction in your life.

I taught them, if nothing else, go to His word at random! This means to open the bible at random and read the chapter. A verse of scripture just might jump out at you. Even if it's not clear on what was read, ask the Lord for understanding and usually He gives it to you through His Spirit.

Someone might say something in conjunction with your situation or the circumstances on your mind, and they don't even know anything about them. Most people call it a coincidence! Someone will say something to you, and your response is, "It's funny, I was just thinking about doing that, or going there, or getting one of those!"

That's exactly what I did when my niece approached me about going to my mother's home town to share the word of the Lord. I went to the Lord over the matter after returning home from the holidays. During my search in the scriptures, I was given a passage of scripture in 2 Kings 15, verses 32-35, which reads:

"In the second year of Pekah son of Remaliah king of Israel, Jotham son of Uzziah king of Judah began to reign. He was twenty five years old when he became king, and he reigned in Jerusalem sixteen years. His mother's name was Jerusha daughter of Zadok. He did what was right in the eyes of the Lord, just as

his father Uzziah had done. The high places, however, were not removed the people continued to offer sacrifices and burn incense there. Jotham rebuilt the Upper Gate of the temple of the Lord."   *(2 Kings 15:32-35 NIV)*

As far as my search of direction in my life, I got no direction whatsoever upon my search of scripture in God's word. Instead, I got curious about what I had just read. I went from looking for direction and guidance into curiosity. I simply asked the Lord, "What does the 'Upper Gate' represent? And what is the 'Upper Gate?' In my search through the scriptures, I was led to 2 Chronicles 27:3, which read:

"Jotham rebuilt the "Upper Gate" of the temple of the Lord and did extensive work on the wall at the hill of Ophel."   *(2 Chronicles 27:3 NIV)*

Now I was on a mission to find out what the Lord God was trying to tell me out of His own heart. I was still trying to figure out if it had anything to do with my niece's request for me to share the word of God in the area she and my mother live.

As I searched the scriptures, I came to find out that the 'Upper Gate' of the temple was situated in the northern part of the temple that stood during that time in the bible. It is actually the gate of the inner and upper court room to the temple. The wall of Ophel is the southern gate to the temple of God during the time frame of Jotham, the righteous King.

I sat and wondered, is this my sign I was looking for in guidance and direction for my life? My niece and my mother literally live south of my hometown where I resided. So, impulsively, I think it's ok to go in that direction to share God's word in that region. But instead of getting excited and convinced to go that way, I was left puzzled by the work on 'the Upper Gate' which is the northern part of the temple, the gate to the inner and upper court. I live north of my mother and my niece, so do I stay put?

I was questioning it, because in my own search of wanting to know what the upper gate was in reference to the temple, I came across God's own written word that Jotham, the same righteous King in the book of 2 Kings, did extensive work on the wall of Ophel located in the same area of the south gate of the temple in the book of 2 Chronicles. I even took it upon myself to go search diagrams found in bibles to see what the temple looked like in different time frames of the bible: Ezekiel's temple, David's temple, Solomon's temple, and even the temple in Jesus Christ's time.

This didn't help, and I got confused. Once confusion hit me, I knew I was in enemy territory. I know that God's word tells me,

"For God is not a God of disorder but of peace, as in all the congregations of the saints."   *(1 Corinthians 14:33 NIV)*

As well as I know that passage of scripture by heart, and the truth implicated through it, the latter portion of that passage has always puzzled me. If he is the God of peace, and not confusion, why is there no peace among the congregation of his saints?

In a way, I know why but, that was not what I was searching for when I began. Thus saying, I know why it is written: judgment begins in the house of God! That was where I left my thoughts and search of guidance with God as far as going somewhere to share his word.

A few days had passed since the day I was on a search mission for guidance in my life. During that particular weekend, I went out of town to visit one of my daughters at her apartment. In my time alone, after my daughter and my wife went shopping, I went to the word of God as I usually do because I want to literally hear something from the Lord. This I do, not knowing if I will get a word, or not!

Still looking for guidance and direction from the week before, Jeremiah 51:11-12 jumped out at me! It reads:

"Sharpen the arrows, take up the shields! The Lord has stirred up the Kings of the Medes, because his purpose is to destroy the temple of Babylon. The Lord will take vengeance, vengeance for his temple. Lift up a banner against the walls of Babylon! Reinforce the guard, station the watchmen, prepare an ambush! The Lord will carry out his purpose, his decree against the people of Babylon."

(Jeremiah 51:11-12 NIV)

That was totally far-fetched from what I had been searching for from the Lord a few days earlier looking for direction and guidance in my life. I had already given it over to the Lord, yet it still hung over my spirit, only because of the sincerity and inner hunger for Jesus Christ in niece's voice.

My mind was already made up by the very first passage of scripture I had read when all this began: 2 Kings 15:32-35. Jotham the righteous King did extensive work on the upper room gate, which was located on the north gate, being the gate entrance into the inner courts of the temple. Being located north of my niece by where she lives, I had a notion I was to go nowhere in this time frame of my life. But in the midst of this search of guidance, I realized extensive work needed to be done on the upper gate room.

This hunger of revelation just kept going on in me about what the Lord was trying to show me. The only reason it carried on was because I kept hearing my niece's voice and sincerity, not to mention the look on her face from the hunger of wanting to know more of Jesus Christ than she already does.

I wasn't questioning God it was my compassion and love for my niece. But I am one who has NEVER let a family member very close to me side track me from God's guidance and direction in my life, not even my mom, or my beloved wife. Even though they are the greatest and most God given inspirational women in my life, they cannot, and will not, change my dedicated heart to God's will in my life. That itself is a story I could share to build one's faith in trusting the Lord your God with your whole heart.

After reading Jeremiah 51:11-12 at my daughter's apartment the Spirit of the Lord began to stir me up. I didn't know what it was, but I would soon find out.

Chapter 2 - Vision of a Compass

"The Lord makes firm the steps of the one who delights in Him though he may stumble, he will not fall, for the Lord upholds Him with his hand."

(Psalm 37:23-24 NIV)

Days had already turned into weeks following my niece's request as I pondered the whole case scenario of what was stirring in the atmospheric realms of God. I was already convinced that it had nothing to do with me going to another town to share His word. Though it started with guidance for direction in my life over it, it led me on a scripture search for answers to what the Lord meant by saying, "He was going take vengeance for his temple."

As I just mentioned, I thoroughly searched through biblical temple diagram drawings in the bibles I use in studying the word of God. Since it led me nowhere, I had already given it up as far as the temple of God was concerned. I went from wondering how God was going to take vengeance for His temple, to why He would recommend us to take up our shields while sharpening our arrows.

I was at home in my workshop doing my thing. I am a full time woodworking craftsman. I live on the band saw, doing what I love to do: cutting out wood letters and shapes people can use and paint as arts and craft projects. One particular day while doing my normal thing, cutting letters out of wood on my band saw, I was very intently listening with my heart and my spirit as I always do to see if I could get some kind of revelation of what was actually going on in the Spirit realm of God.

The atmosphere of the heavenly realms was moving nonstop. I could feel the waging and combat of war between evil and good in the heavenly realms around me, in me and above me. I was trying to grasp the reason for it. I was in a rhythm of doing my work, when all of a sudden the Lord gave me a vision.

He showed me a compass one uses for direction and guidance. I looked at the compass very intently when the Lord asked me, "What do you see?" I said, "A compass." At this point, my band saw was still running. He said, "You have seen correctly!"

Then He asked, "What else do you see?" I said, "A compass!" He said, "Did you not see the letters on the compass? The letters N, S, E and W?"

I said, "I do now that you pointed them out to me!" Then He asked me, "What do those letters signify to the person using that compass?" I answered, "The direction one is going while using that compass." "You have answered correctly," He said!

Then I was shown the needle pointer on the compass. I saw myself holding it in my hand as I watched the needle swivel from "W," to "N," to "E." I noticed it never swiveled to the letter "S," on the compass. I then moved with the compass facing myself towards the south where I stood and live. It was the south side of my residential property. It was then that the needle moved towards the letter "S".

As soon as it did, the Lord then showed me a transparent image of His Son, Jesus Christ, as He was left hanging on the cross. I could still see the compass through Him. It was as though the cross, and the crucified body of our Lord and Savior, Jesus Christ, had the compass embedded between them. The Lord's head was positioned on the "N" part of the compass, while both his hands were positioned over the "E" and "W" part of the compass, while his feet laid over the "S" part of the compass.

I begin to cry so hard, I had to turn my band saw off! My sorrow overtook my body where I couldn't even concentrate on cutting the shapes of wood. The sorrow just increased to where I had to leave my work area and go inside my house. It was then that my sorrow turned into great mourning and wailing.

I went into my house to play inspirational prayer music as I wept and prayed unto the Lord over the vision He was giving me. As I wept, He said, "You were so curious about what the temple looked like that I was going to take vengeance for, and what the upper gate was, and is, right along with the wall of Ophel on the southern part of the temple. Now you have seen it! Or did you forget what you have read in my book?"

"I did not see a temple in the city, because the Lord God Almighty and the Lamb are its temple."   *(Revelation 21:22 NIV)*

I wept, and wept, and wept until I fell asleep from being drained out spiritually by God in heaven, showing me His love for mankind, who doesn't even seem to notice it! Those that do see it as a free token to heaven one can use when they die here in earth.

I passed out from the sorrow that plagued my soul. It was hours later that I awoke from my sleep. I woke up trying not to cry from the sorrow that came forth from heaven in the vision God had given me over His temple: the temple of Jesus Christ, our Lord and Savior, *"...the Lamb of God, slain from the creation of the world."*
(Revelation 13:8 NIV)

But we all know the feeling of having seen one of our loved ones get hurt, broken, or even murdered by someone else in their life. You try and move on, yet the image of our loved one getting hurt and violated lingers on. This is the best way I can describe this vision given to me by God in heaven over His Son, Jesus Christ! Yet to my great amazement, God the Father wasn't angry when he showed me the vision! He started crying like we do from broken heartedness!

It was as though HE, God my Father, was crying **in** me and **through** me before I passed out. I could hear Him asking Himself, what did I do wrong to deserve this? What could I have done to make it different? Why didn't I see this coming from those I created with My own hands to love and cherish Me throughout eternity? Will anyone ever see Me for who I really am? Does anyone really care in this heartless world of humanity that I created?

Yet in the midst of all these questions of humanity going through the spiritual realm I was in after waking up, I heard a very faint voice cry out from the vision:

"My God, my God, why have you forsaken me?"   *(Matthew 27:46 NIV)*

I then realized why the temple, the Lamb of God, was forsaken! It had been adorned with our selfish gods and idols. That's when darkness came over the land. God would not put up with our ignorance anymore towards Him and the sacrificed Lamb He had provided unto the salvation of our souls.

In other words, people think, 'Do as you please, and want, because once saved, always saved!' Really? Then why do I read a passage of scripture in the Bible we all believe in that reads:

"Anyone whose name was not found written in the book of life was thrown into the lake of fire."   *(Revelation 20:15 NIV)*

That would mean your name that was once there when you truly and whole heartedly loved God through Jesus Christ has been blotted out. Why?

"And I saw the dead, small and great, stand before God and the books were opened: and another book was opened, which is the book of Life: and the dead

were judged out of those things which were written in the books, according to their works. And the sea gave up the dead which were in it and death and hell delivered up the dead which were in them: and they were judged according to their works. And death and hell were cast into the lake of fire. This is the second death. And whosoever was not found written in the book of life was cast into the lake of fire. (Revelation 20:12-15 NIV)

So, yes! God was up to something in showing me the vision of the compass with the Lamb of God on it, slain from the foundations of the world, with regards to his people. For some reason or another, I knew it wasn't going to be pretty, what I was about to be shown and told. In fact, I knew I was going to be told something I didn't want to hear. But being I live my life for Him, rather than myself, I was ready and obedient to listen and eat the scroll from God's hands.

Need a better example or explanation on what I was spiritually enduring? As a kid you know you're in trouble and you have a spanking waiting for you. You try and play it off as though everything is normal, yet it's not! It's still coming!

"Because the Lord disciplines the one he loves, and chastens everyone he accepts as his son." (Hebrews 12:6 NIV)

Chapter 3 - Destroy this Temple

"Jesus answered them, Destroy this temple, and I will raise it again in three days. The Jews replied, It has taken forty-six years to build this temple, and you are going to raise it in three days? But the temple he had spoken of was his body. After he was raised from the dead, his disciples recalled what he had said. Then they believed the scripture and the words that Jesus had spoken."

(John 2:19-22 NIV)

I started on a mission of guidance and direction for my life from the Lord from a particular encounter I had just a few weeks earlier. I got His guidance, but not what I was looking for. I ended up being led to God's agenda for this world in the very near coming days, in the very near future. Actually, I would say, we are in that time frame now. It is an agenda that is going to affect every single life on the face of this earth.

Vengeance for His temple! It had totally become the main topic of concern the Lord God of heaven was sharing with me after my search efforts for guidance and direction in my life. I knew this whole case scenario had become a message for me to share with His people. It had nothing to do with me going anywhere to share His word, other than my tablet which will then be published into book form.

I was now intently soul searching for answers to what the Lord meant by His saying:

"Sharpen your arrows, and take up your shield! For a battle cry has come from ON HIGH!"   *(Isaiah 51:11-12)*

To me personally, it couldn't have meant any more to me than when the Lord says in His word to us for our everyday life of living.

"Finally, be strong in the Lord and in his mighty power. Put on the full armor of God, so that you can take your stand against the devil's schemes. For our struggle is not against flesh and blood, but against the rulers, against authorities, against the powers of this dark world and against the spiritual forces of evil in heavenly realms. Therefore put on the full Armor of God, so that when the day of evil comes, you may be able to stand your ground, and after you have done everything to stand. Stand firm then, with the belt of truth buckled around your waist, with the breastplate of righteousness in place and with your feet fitted with readiness that comes from the gospel of peace. In addition to all this, take up the shield of faith, with which you can extinguish all the flaming arrows of the evil one. Take the helmet of salvation and the sword of the Spirit, which is the word of God!"

(Ephesians 6:12-17 NIV)

Being a prophet of the Lord, I knew what He was about to tell me was futuristic, even though it applies to the now. What does it mean, other than what it says? "I will tell you what it means says the Lord! You are taught to stand on My word with the armor I, the Lord your God, have provided all of you with in this life you live. Most of you are not even aware of the armor that is yours just for the asking, in Jesus' Name, much less its full potential impact the armor can provide for you," says the Lord!

"I see many followers of my Son, Christ Jesus, use His armor to protect themselves against the devil's schemes in the life they live in me, and through me. Yet I see only ONE problem from my perspective with my Jesus Christ followers. The majority of my Jesus Christ followers use their faith and rituals as **THEIR** armor of God. In other words, they're content with going to church once, or maybe twice a week, and having faith in me God. They set aside maybe one day, or two days they give me, the Lord your God through church, and the rest of the week is theirs. Not to mention the two days they do give me consist of maybe six hours at the most between the two of them combined. If even that! So who does the rest of the week belong to? You, or me, the Lord your God you supposedly serve?"

"What about when Satan turns it on? In other words, you are stretched beyond your own strength of power and resources, and even your faith. In other words, your six hours to me, and your beautiful church wardrobes you wear into my presence, are nothing more than a joke to Satan as he laughs his butt off at you and your psychological attitude towards me, the Lord your God in heaven. He, the devil, laughs at you, and even insults you with sarcastic remarks like he did others in the bible that are written for you to see, and read about so you won't be like them. But do you read it? Probably not! Well this is what I am talking about," says the Lord!

"Some Jews who went around driving out evil spirits **TRIED** *to invoke the name of the Lord Jesus over those who were demon possessed. They would say, In the name of Jesus whom Paul preaches, I command you to come out. Seven sons of Sceva, a Jewish chief priest, were doing this. One day the evil spirit answered them, Jesus I know, and Paul I know about,* **but who are you?** *Then the man who had the evil spirit jumped on them and overpowered them all. He gave them such a beating that they ran out of the house naked and bleeding."*

(Acts 19:13-16 NIV)

"That's how you do me with your religious psychological faiths. You invoke the evil spirits through your measly ritual sacrifice of church and religions. So the evil spirits in turn jump back on you after your watered down prayers of forgiveness and sacrifice are made through your ritual hourly sacrifices to me. They just wait outside for you to leave your manmade temples where they in turn never left you."

"Can you actually see that? ***The evil spirits you entertain in your life go to church with you!*** But as you arrive in church, they stay outside waiting for you. They know you are not at all sincere in your faith towards Me, the Lord your God, Who created you in His image."

"Then there are some evil spirits that literally live *inside you* that go into your services with you while in my presence. That's why you sit there on your pews, looking around to see who is wearing what in comparison to what you are wearing. They entertain you, looking at someone you know has issues that you know they need to get rid of, since they are not perfect like you. The evil spirits bore the hell out of you, while agitating you through hunger pains, trying to decide what restaurant to eat at after the service is over. So you turn to your cell phone and social media amidst the service you are attending."

"Then your patience pays off as the time of the end of your sacrifice to me comes to an end. They, the evil spirits, know you are more than ready to get out of there and this part of your weekly sacrifice. That's why they use carnal hunger pains within you to get you to decide where to go to enjoy your carnal appetite."

"And the evil spirits that you entertain in your life are more than happy that your ritual sacrifice is over with, as they wait for you outside. That is why the evil spirits of this world overpower you and give you such a beating leaving you naked and bleeding."

"You ever felt naked even though you had clothes on? Of course you have! That feeling overcomes you when you have lost everything to your addictions of drugs and alcohol! You have lost everything to an unfaithful partner who literally destroyed you, ripping your heart to shreds."

"Your mom and dad literally ripped the word "life" out of your vocabulary, leaving you trying to figure out what life really is. You don't even know what that means because of what you are seeing with your own eyes. Being sexually molested has left you feeling dirty and ashamed of yourself, though very few notice it. But you want to continue giving yourself over to those evil spirits instead of me," says the Lord!

"No wonder the evil spirits have your heart bleeding. I am the God of heaven, and your creator, and I really belong in your heart where my kingdom really should be. It is then that I would heal your bleeding, broken hearts. But since I am not in your heart as I should be, you go to church thinking you are going to find ME there. That is why you go way out of your way in dressing up thinking you will impress me, the Lord your God with your looks, while the whole time I am looking at your hypocrite hearts. You really think your wardrobe is going to stop the bleeding of your broken heart? Does it even skim the surface of drying your tears from your cheeks as you fight the pain of broken heartedness? I didn't think so!"

"That is why Satan attacks you the way he does! And what do you do? You fight it all week long, while suffering the affliction and persecution of Satan, and mental torture while waiting for the next church service day to see if you can find some spiritual release of your tormented spirit."

"Am I, the Lord your God, mocking church? NO! Go if you want! Praise me all you want! I love it when you truly worship me and praise me," says the Lord! "You ought to try and praise me, and worship me all the days, and hours of your life. In my Love, I am trying to give you heads up in the days that are up ahead for you, because I truly love you with **ALL MY** heart."

"That is why you would need to sharpen your arrows, and take up your shields more seriously than you already do. Actually what I, the Lord your God, am doing in this day and age, and even at this very moment is, I am sharing these words with you because I am building an army of relentless soldiers who will not sway to the left, or to the right in their walk with my Son, Jesus Christ. Those who can hear my Spirit with their God given ears. Those are the ones led of the Spirit of God!"

"Whether you turn to the right or to the left, your ears will hear a voice behind you, saying, This is the way; walk in it."   (Isaiah 30:21 NIV)

"Soldiers who are on call 24/7! Just waiting for an assignment, or command from their God in heaven! Warriors for Christ! Not even a thought of compromising in his true devoted followers whatsoever. On their knees and in prayer the whole time they are awake, whether in the evening, or at midnight, or when the rooster crows, or at dawn. Always on watch!"

"The word of the Lord is what it is, and no one will ever change it. So if you are going to use My word as a defense mechanism in your life, then act on my word and believe what you profess through your action of the word of God in your life. Not just mere words you say, and know! Even the devils believe in me, the Lord your God!"

"Let's use a talented individual as an example. They're good at what they do just through the gift given to them by God. Especially in sports! But if they don't sharpen their skills in the gift they have, what use is the gift given to them of God? They don't practice, they feel they're good enough to not worry about competing, etc., etc. Even as talented as they are, they have to earn their spot on the roster to the team they are competing for and representing."

"Likewise, eternal life, that I the Lord your God have given you through my Son, Jesus Christ, is something many of you followers rest your lives and spirits on in a future tense. That's great you are convinced of where you are going once you pass from this life to the next. However, one who has eternal life in the bag already can also believe God heals according to the same word that promises eternal life."

"Then at the same time of having such faith, they lose a loved one through a sickness God supposedly didn't heal. Then what? You believe in God's word, don't you? You are saved, through your gift God gave you through his Son, Jesus Christ, right? So your response to the loss of a loved one according to your faith in the gift God gave you of eternal life through his Son, Jesus Christ would be, or should be:

"And we know that in all things God works for the good of those who love Him, and who have been called according to his purpose." (Romans 8:28 NIV)

"This holds true especially in relationships that I established in creation, such as marriage and family. You trust in my written word in those relationships, right? Yet, divorce rules and dominates the lives you live. Betrayal is very common in what you consider family amidst those you would least expect it from. It is written for you!

"A man's enemies will be the members of his own household."
(Matthew 10:36 NIV)

"Broken heartedness rules the hearts and lives of my broken people," says the Lord! "In the midst of great accomplishment, or a marriage, a family, siblings and relatives, and relationships, Satan with more reason raises his ugly head in the midst of such happiness in one's life from one least expected. That is why it is also written for you!"

"The Lord Almighty is with us, the God of Jacob is our fortress."
(Psalm 46:11 NIV)

Trust in the Lord with all your heart and lean not on your own understanding. In all thy ways acknowledge Him, and he shall direct thy paths."
(Proverbs 3:5-6 NIV)

"But that's not the usual response I get from my followers who believe in me so much, says the Lord! Instead, I get angry, hurting children who then turn to rebellion toward Me for a prayer not being answered as they thought it should have been. Yet they hold onto their eternal life, while being consumed through a spirit of anger and confusion towards me, the God you believe in so much."

"If you had sharpened your skills before the loss of a loved one ever came your way, or before that loved one was even born for that matter, your grieving would be something the Lord could heal you from. Then He could make you a light of hope to others who are going through the same valley of sorrow and broken heartedness as you are."

"If you had sharpened your arrows and taken up your shield before family ever came into your life, or relationships ever entered into your social realm of life, it would not have made you lose hope through anger and disappointment," says the Lord! "That only comes by being a soldier servant of the Lord, by staying in the word of God, and while being aware of what God has said in His word about life."

"One minute you are here amidst your loved ones, the next minute you're not. That goes for relationships too! One minute your soul mate is your knight in shining armor, or your princess in an elegant dress of love and beauty. The next minute, he or she is your worst nightmare from hell. I don't wish that on anybody, but I see it on a continual basis in the lives you live," says the Lord! "It is one of Satan's greatest tools - turning people against me," says the Lord.

"I didn't do anything! I don't control my people like robots, like you do you snake. You are the coward I am after, the one that I defeated by the way of the cross through My Son. In My realm of the spirit, Satan, you were defeated! But in the religious, and complacent spirit of Christianity you haven't been."

"That is why I am rousing up my sons and daughters who are willing to listen and give heed to my command. Take up your shields and sharpen your arrows," says the Lord!

"Why, you do not even know what will happen tomorrow. What is your life? You are a mist that appears for a little while and then vanishes." (James 4:14 NIV)

"That wasn't part of your faith in your time of praying for a healing for your loved one, was it? That wasn't in your realm of faith in asking me to save your marriage either, or your children, or your very own life for that matter. Even with that knowledge of the word, it doesn't take the sorrow and anguish away that comes from losing a loved one, does it?"

"If anything, what it does is this: it stops Satan by not allowing his spirits of anger and confusion towards me, the Lord your God, to move in on you. It's called commitment to me, the Lord your God!"

"Why am I using this subject of a loved one unexpectedly and suddenly being gone in one's life marriage, or even in social relationships? Because of what is about to take place in your world you live in, more than it already does, and has: Terrorism! Evil acts and outbursts of random radicals who want nothing of me," says the Lord!

"It has become a fact of life as thousands upon thousands, if not millions, of innocent lives have suffered from this onslaught of hell on humanity. It has become a form of oppression on the minds of *my people*, whether it's fear, or expectation of its next target, and location. That is the meaning of my word you read: *The Lord has stirred up the Kings of the Medes."*   *(Jeremiah 51:11 NIV)*

If you personally begin a search on who the kings of the Medes were at that given time in Jeremiah's day, interestingly enough, you would found out the Medes are the ancestors of the modern day Kurds. The Kurds are middle easterners in this present day and age that reside in Turkey, Iran, northern Iraq, and northern Syria. Not at all surprising!

So, what would you think if you knew the Lord is doing this, and allowing it to happen? He is allowing the enemy, through terrorism, to get a message across to His people that they do not know the day, nor the hour, of the coming of the Son of Man.

"In their own personal lives, this should put a little fear and respect in *my people* towards Me, their Father which art in heaven. The fear I speak of is more of a respect towards Me, God in heaven."

But guess what? I guess it doesn't go that way, does it? Because terrorism isn't from God! No, it's not!

"I just allow it for one purpose: to fulfill My word that no one knows the day, nor the hour, of the coming of the Son of Man in their own personal life."

So, God is behind terrorism? No! The devil is! You people have literally forgotten this world is Satan's, haven't you? What? Yes, it's his world!

"You don't remember? He tried giving it to me, your Lord and Savior, before I even started my mission on this earth. After fasting forty days, I was hungry! He knew I was! Literally hungry! Just like a lot of you are in the spiritual sense. You crave the things of this world. Your appetite of gratification is never satisfied. I had just told the coward, Satan, man does not live on bread alone, but by the word of God! So what does he do? What he does to all of you! Look for yourself what he did to me, your Lord and Savior, Jesus Christ!"

"The devil led Him up to a high place and showed Him in an instant ALL the kingdoms of the world. And he said to Him, 'I will give you all their authority and splendor it has been given to me, and I can give it to anyone I want to. If you worship me, it will all be yours.' Jesus answered, 'It is written: Worship the Lord your God and serve Him only.'" (Luke 4:5-8 NIV)

"You see what my Son responded with? Worship the Lord your God, and serve Him ONLY! But what do you do? You worship religions and self-wills. You worship celebrity idols of all types. You desire more materialistic things than you do my presence in your life," says the Lord!

"So, Satan gives you his kingdoms of this world that consist of addictions, anger, hatred, racism, religions, denominations, rituals, customs, perversion and gods of gold, silver, wood and stone. Need I go on? That is why Jesus Christ continually told the people: be on watch, be alert! For you don't know when I will come."

That's one purpose why the enemy is allowed to do his thing: to fulfill God's destination date with you in eternity. It's a very ugly thought that I would even say that. But what can you do when the enemy strikes unannounced through terrorist attacks?

The other reason God is allowing the kings of the Medes to do their thing is to fulfill what the Lord just gave you in Jeremiah 51:11 -- to destroy Babylon! The terrorists have but one mission in their quest, and that is to conquer the world, and get the message out that their god of religion is the one that is to be worshipped.

It's a war of power and control over the nations of the world. It's this way, or no way! Believe in the god we serve, or die in the process. If you are asking me, it's another form of an anti-Christ spirit ruling in this world we live in, minus the anti-Christ Himself in the picture. We are all aware of an anti-Christ that is coming into the world with the intentions of establishing a one world government system that is basically setting itself up already right underneath your noses.

"It will be powered by worshipping its leader through a religious kingdom that will be established by one man's power in authority. He will be the messiah that the world has anxiously been waiting for in establishing world peace and unity. He will establish a world peace that not even Jesus Christ, being the true God, eternal God, was ever able to establish.

"Of course Jesus Christ never came to establish peace on earth, but to give peace and joy to his faithful followers to help them overcome the darkness in the world they live in. That was why He told His disciples:

"Peace I leave with you; my peace I give you. I do not give to you as the world

gives. Do not let your hearts be troubled and do not be afraid."

(John 14:27 NIV)

I prophesy and decree these very same words to you, in this very day, hour, and moment in your life, right now! Why? Because of what you are about to read in this God-given message to you in helping you build up your faith in the Lord for the days ahead.

"A faith and knowledge resting on the hope of eternal life, which God, who does not lie, promised before the beginning of time."   *(Titus 1:2 NIV)*

"As the rain and the snow come down from heaven, and do not return to it without watering the earth making it bud and flourish, so that it yields seed for the sower and bread for the eater, so is my word that goes out from my mouth: It will not return to me empty, but will accomplish what I desire and achieve the purpose for which I sent it."   *(Isaiah 55:10-11 NIV)*

"Therefore, my purpose to destroy Babylon will be accomplished through the kings of the Medes. Most of you are not even aware of the kingdom of Babylon that is in your faces, are you? What is Babylon to most of you? Babylon is a historic event that has already taken place in your past history. It rose to world power and dominance, only to be conquered, destroyed and left in ruins," says the Lord!

"But now I have a Babylonian empire that has raised its ugly head of power in my very face," says the Lord! "Though it is not visible to the naked eye, its power to influence and affect people's lives by the millions is very obvious."

"The entrance to the original Babylon empire that once existed, but now lies in ruins, was called 'the gate of God', or 'gates of Gods'. This Babylonian empire that exists now, though you can't see it with the naked eye, has the same name inscribed on its gates: the gates of God!"

"Then the angel carried me away in the Spirit into a desert. There I saw a woman sitting on a scarlet beast that was covered with blasphemous names and had seven heads and ten horns. The woman was dressed in purple and scarlet, and was glittering with gold, precious stones and pearls. She had a golden cup in her hand, filled with abominable things and the filth of her adulteries. The name written on her forehead was a mystery: BABYLON THE GREAT THE MOTHER OF PROSTITUTES AND OF THE ABOMINATIONS OF THE EARTH."

(Revelation 17:3-5 NIV)

Futuristically speaking, the Babylon Empire is coming back into existence with its world ruler that will be seen as the anti-Christ. But most of you are aware of that, whether you were taught about it, or have heard about it, or even read about it.

"I AM not concerned at all about future events that are headed your way, says the Lord! I AM more concerned about your personal future existence in eternity than I am your future in this world you live in."

"Your future in this world you live has only two outcomes. You either die when I call you home, or I come in the clouds to get *my people* who are waiting for my return. That's it!"

"Where you end up in eternity is my main concern for you, *my people,* either way. This Babylon that I am talking about is not even called Babylon. It just represents the Babylonian Empire through the works of the spirits it consist of."

"It's the Babylonian Empire called RELIGION, which consists of so many names of religions, faiths, denominations and beliefs…these are the gates of God that you make as entrances into my kingdom of heaven."

"How dare you build an empire such as that in my face," says the Lord, "when you know very well what my Son, Jesus Christ, told all of you:

"I am the Gate. Whoever enters through me will be saved. He will come in and go out, and find pasture."   *(John 10:9 NIV)*

"And if you are one who didn't know that, now you do! I am not talking only to a lost world here, but also all my followers who have set their own gates of religion and faith gods before me."

"Very truly I tell you Pharisees, anyone who does not enter the sheep pen by the gate, but climbs in by some other way, is a thief and a robber. The one who enters by the gate is the shepherd of the sheep."   *(John 10:1-2 NIV)*

"But now you have been told! I have my followers who follow me only with words, and no deeds. They confess and claim they have eternal life in my Son, yet they hold onto their faiths, religions and their righteous deeds that are done before men - to be seen by men - according to their faith and beliefs. Yet, they have no change of heart towards others, and even me, the Lord their God in heaven. They still can't stand a different skin colored person from them. They still won't forgive those who offended them! They still elevate their righteous living over others who don't even measure up to their status quo of righteous living."

"Listen to this: there was a man dressed in a white robe who was a Shepherd. He came before a very large crowd with a very large pitcher, with crystal clear water in it. The crowd consisted of very thirsty people who were enduring the heat of the moment in their lives. Their moments consisted of situations that were way beyond their control, while others were in situations that had them with their backs against the wall."

"Many made drastic decisions in dealing with their situations that left them with total regret for doing what they should not have done. These had total regret within their soul and being, wishing they could take it back, and start all over again. This caused their souls to dry out from regret and guilt within."

"They were in need of a soul-thirst quenching remedy - a total quenching of the dryness within their soul and spirit:

"On the last and greatest day of the feast, Jesus stood and said in a loud voice, If anyone is thirsty, let Him come to me and drink. Whoever believes in me, as the scripture has said, streams of living water will flow from within Him. By this he meant the Spirit, whom those who believe in Him were later to receive. Up to that time the Spirit had not yet been given, since Jesus had not yet been glorified. On hearing his words, some of the people said, Surely this man is the Prophet. Others said, He is the Christ. Still others asked, How can the Christ come from Galilee? Does not the scripture say that the Christ will one from David's family and from Bethlehem, the town where David lived?" (John 7:37-42 NIV)

"At the same moment as the man who stood in the white robe among the suffering people, there stood another man in a very fancy, flowing colored robe. He spoke up in the midst of the confusion of the people, saying the very same words the man in the white robe had said. 'If a man is thirsty, let Him come to me and drink!' Unlike the shepherd in the white robe who only had one pitcher of crystal clear water, this other man had several pitchers full of water. He even had flavored packs in front of his pitchers, thus giving the people a choice of what flavor they desired to quench their thirst with an additive taste."

"Thus the people were divided because of Jesus. Some wanted to seize Him, but no one laid a hand on Him." (John 7:43-44 NIV)

"Then each went to his own home." (John 7:53 NIV)

"But Jesus went to the Mount of Olives." (John 8:1 NIV)

"In the name of 'personal choice', all my people left the man in the white robe. They went home while choosing their own flavor of desired religious names and self-wills over the <u>ONLY</u> name given in heaven unto man that can quench one's soul, thus leading them unto salvation. As far as the man standing in the white robe: *Therefore God exalted Him to the highest place and gave Him the name that is above every name."* (Philippians 2:9 NIV)

"Upon being rejected of his thirst-quenching water, my Son, Jesus Christ, went to the Mount of Olives. Have you ever wondered for what? You should read My word more often than you do, and you would learn more about My Son's life. You have no clue what he endured for all of you, even before the cross and crucifixion that led Him to His death. You should make it a habit to go to my word in search of my Son's will for mankind. You would find out, *'But Jesus often withdrew to lonely places and prayed.'"* (Luke 5:16 NIV)

"Not just for your self-interest and needs, but for the will of God your Father in heaven to be done on earth as it is in heaven for mankind. *'In those days, Jesus went out to the mountain to pray, and he spent the night in prayer to God.'*" (Luke 12:6 NIV)

"You wouldn't believe me if I told you how many countless times my Son spent sorrowfully praying for you, His child, out of His genuine love He has for you, even unto this day. Even now, to this very day and age, He intercedes for you *my people*, unlike the man in the fancy suit who receives his wages from you, his faithful religious followers. This one is always making sure the collection buckets are passed out before even giving you a message. When did my Son look for handouts? All He looked for were people like you who needed a touch of healing and forgiveness in their lives."

"Who then is the one who condemns? No one. Christ Jesus who died – more than that, who was raised to life – is at the right hand of God and is also interceding for us." (Romans 8:34 NIV)

"My Son continually makes intercession for you, *my people*. But to what avail? The cross He endured for the sins of the world opened the door of heaven unto the salvation of mankind. But who cares? Church going is your remedy unto salvation! But let a prostitute come through your church doors and watch your reactions. Let a drug addict, or a homosexual, or a trans-sexual walk through that door. How would you act?"

"My Son had to endure His cross of love for you in order for you to obtain eternal life in Me," says the Lord! "So you think it won't cost you anything to get where you're going? Really? To go anywhere in this life you live, doesn't it cost you something? We're not talking money, either. We are talking everyday living: going to work, going to the food stamp office since you don't want to work, whether by foot, or a vehicle for transportation."

"If nothing else, it costs you time, whether you earn your keep by working at your job, or it costs you time out of your day to go looking for handouts since you don't care to work, you free loading spirit! Even you drug and alcohol addicted people who stand by the roadways, taking advantage of generous people who gave, who have now become hard hearted in their generosity because of you. You addicts have got to hustle your next move, to earn or steal your money, to get your next high on drugs or alcohol."

"Are you mocking your people Lord? Mocking? No! I am only telling you what I see on a consistent basis, day in, and day out in my peoples' lives that makes me wish they would put that kind of effort toward me, the Lord their God, in finding their happiness and contentment in me. That is why it is written for all of you:

"Then Jesus said to his disciples, Whoever wants to be my disciple must deny themselves and take up their cross and follow me."
(Matthew 16:24; Mark 8:34; Luke 14:27 NIV)

"I know your deeds. See, I have placed an open door that no one can shut. I know you have little strength, yet you have kept my word and have not denied my name."
(Revelation 3:8 NIV)

"But for those of you who deny My name, even though you say you

THIS

believe, I say unto you, Look!"

"After this I looked, and behold, a door standing open in heaven! And the first voice which I heard, like the sound of a (war) *trumpet speaking with me, said, Come up here, and I will show you what must take place after these things."*
(Revelation 4:1 AMP)

"If you have ever wondered why all you ever see and encounter is opposition in your quest of living an upright life towards me, the Lord your God in heaven, your answer would be: you are a marked target of Satan, who has but one goal on his mind: to take you into outer darkness, into his kingdom, where there will be weeping and gnashing of teeth."

"In fact, everyone who wants to live a godly life in Christ Jesus will be persecuted."
(2 Timothy 3:12 NIV)

"In fact the very same Jesus Christ you believe in, and put your whole heart and faith toward, said,

"Then you will be handed over to be persecuted and put to death, and you will be hated by all nations **<u>BECAUSE OF ME.</u>** *At that time many will turn away from their faith and will betray and hate each other."*
(Matthew 24:9-10 NIV)

"Why? Because you, along with everybody else, are not willing to take up their shields, or sharpen their arrows."

Chapter 4 - North Gate

For, as I have often told you before and now say again even with tears, many live as enemies of the cross of Christ. Their destiny is destruction, their god is their stomach, and their glory is their shame. Their mind is on earthly things.

(Philippians 3:18-19 NIV)

You can look all around you and see what this passage of God's word is in reference to, can't you? People living it up as best as they know how; doing everything they want, how they want, even if it's against their own conscience, knowing they shouldn't be doing what they are doing. This is totally contrary to what God's word says about living your life in the presence of the Lord your God, Who created you. Why? Because your god is your stomach!

What exactly does that mean? It means you have a hunger and a drive within you that needs to be satisfied. This hunger is the craving of whatever it is you are feeling, or want and desire out of the life you live. In other words, if you're in the mood for sex, sex it will be! It doesn't matter who it is for some of you, depending on your sexual hormone level, married or not!

"Of course, many think getting or being married solves their lust craving for sex. This is only because they read in My word it is better for one to marry than to burn with passion (see 1 Corinthians 7:9). Being married really doesn't justify your lust even though most of you think it does."

"What? Yes, I am talking about having a relationship with your God in heaven through Jesus Christ. Of course, your minds are more consumed with perversion of the flesh than with an attentive spirit towards me, the Lord your God! The cravings of the carnal being that lives on this earth has nothing to do with your growth and maturity in me, the Lord your God through Jesus Christ."

"Let's say you love Jesus Christ with all your heart, soul and mind, even though you are married. He gives you the peace and joy this world can't give. Not even your marriage gives you that peace! Praise God for the supernatural peace that surpasses all understanding!"

"But, now you're in the mood for sexual passion, a carnal desire that needs fulfilling. So, no problem, right? That's why I have a soul mate! My wife, or my husband! Your marriage partner becomes your carnal desire supplier."

"Now, let's say for some reason or another, your partner isn't interested. Not in the mood? Or, maybe they are sick and bedridden. Now what? Go watch sex movies? Go find another partner? Or, just get royally ticked off from the rejection you encountered from the one you are married to?"

"Now your hope of release to the desires of the flesh has just been shattered. So, instead, you go hang out in a bar, or with friends and do things you normally wouldn't do, just to burn off the steam of your lust and anger with which you are consumed."

"I thought the cross my Son endured for you was your answer to peace, joy, love and happiness in this world you live in," says the Lord. "Why did I use the analogy of sex? Because you live in a perverse world that does nothing more than revolve around that one realm of craving my people have for each other, instead of having a craving to get to know Me, the Lord God of heaven and earth, or who He really is to His people."

"Another reason I used that analogy was to prove a point to you, my followers, who also have cravings of your own: to get what you want out of My written word - to your own ends, through your appetites, leading to destruction. That is your destiny through your carnal appetite: Destruction!"

"That is why you have so many Gospels of my Son, Jesus Christ! You enter through the north gate, through your own wisdom of interpreting and understanding scriptures at your own leisure. You have the gospel of prosperity: "Give and it shall be given unto you, good measure, pressed down and shaken, and running over." What good will it do if you inherit the world and forfeit your soul?"

"Then you have the gospel of healing and miracles, saying, "Lord, we cast out demons in your name, healed the sick, and raised the dead." He said,

"Away from me, you evil doer! I never knew you!"   *(Matthew 7:23)*

"The gospel of encouragement! Never give up, there is always hope! Yet you hate your enemies! I know what my word, teaches you. But you miss the whole concept, the point in all the teachings: you totally ignore the teacher, My Son! All I want to see in you is my Son!"

"Why? Because all your accomplishments, riches and miracles are going to fade one day, and vanish into thin air. So that is why - if you don't stop interpreting scriptures to your own preference of how you think things should be, your glory will be your shame! This means, when you read that many live as enemies to the cross, don't literally put your focus on all the people around you who live lives like you wouldn't ever imagine living. In other words, they are living in sin, and you're not!"

"You are still a sinner by nature in this cursed world you live in. You just found your forgiveness in Me by accepting me into your personal life as your Lord and Savior, Jesus Christ! So be it! Stay focused on me, your Lord and Savior, in order that you won't lose your eternal dwelling with me, the Lord your God."

"Why would I lose my eternal dwelling if I claim you as my Lord and Savior ?"

"What does the cross of My Son, Jesus Christ represent to you, *my people*? Is it a hope of salvation unto eternal life with God in heaven? Is it the symbol of forgiveness unto mankind, courtesy of God their creator who died for the sins of the world so one would have eternal life in heaven? Or, was it just an occurrence that was recorded in a book you call the Bible, with no proof of it to some of you who say GOD doesn't even exist!"

"You say, 'He dies out of Love on a cross for his creation, yet He allows evil, sickness and diseases to plague the world. What kind of God is that? It just doesn't make much sense! Does it?' The reason it doesn't make much sense to you is because you reason with your own human minds that has limits on its thinking ability."

"Have you ever heard, '*The Spirit gives life and the flesh counts for nothing. The words I have spoken to you – they are full of the Spirit and life.*'"

(John 6:63 NIV)

"The cravings of your god - your stomachs - cannot comprehend that! You want answers to feel justified within yourself why things happen the way they do; why God allows evil to flourish, while not answering certain prayers. The only time you go on that mental mission in your life is when it happens to you, or it affects you and no one else. Yet the same thing can happen in other people's lives, and it really isn't a concern to you, and you say, "Well, there isn't anything I can do about it!"

"Really? So, then why, when it does personally affect you, does it make you take up an attitude with me, the Lord your God? You reason in your own realm of life through the lives you live."

"In other words, you believe in eternal life, yet you're stuck mentally in this world with all its dilemmas, while someone you love is dying. This makes you consumed with broken heartedness and anger towards the very God you believe in so much – the One Who has and is the eternal life for which you wait."

"If you then believe in eternal life, why does it kill you inwardly when one gets called home by me out of this world into the world of eternal life?"

"To grieve is one thing, but to take an attitude of anger and resentment towards me, the Lord your God, is another."

"For this reason they could not believe, because, as Isaiah says elsewhere: He has blinded their eyes and hardened their hearts, so they can neither see with their eyes, nor understand with their hearts, nor turn –and I would heal them. Isaiah said this because he saw Jesus' glory and spoke about Him." (John 12:39-41 NIV)

'Which is why My word comes into play in your very own personal life. I will tell you like I did the Pharisees and Sadducees: *"You study the scriptures diligently because you think in them you have eternal life. These are the very scriptures that testify about me. Yet you refuse to come to me to have life."*
(John 5:39-40 NIV)

"Every one of you has a date set in eternity with Me, the Lord your God! In your life, it's called the death of a loved one! I AM the Lord your God, whether you believe in Me or not. Actually, that is why it's very important for you to make your minds up now about who you are going to spend your eternal life with: Me, God your Father in heaven; or Satan, your father the devil. He is the one who consumes your mind with lies and confusion that lead many into outer darkness where there will be weeping and gnashing of teeth."

"Some of you are already there, even though you are very much alive in your body, walking around in this world you live in. You live your life weeping over great sorrows that plague your soul, while gnashing your teeth since you are so consumed with anger. That is why you were told to,

"Do your best to present yourself to God as one approved, a worker who does not need to be ashamed and who correctly handles the word of truth."

(2 Timothy 2:15 NIV)

"The destiny of every living soul ever created of Me, God, that has ever walked the face of this earth you live in has been set for eternity. Where eternity will be spent is left entirely up to you, the individual. But I have set eternity to never be moved. That is why you read,

"As water reflects the face, so one's life reflects the heart. Death and destruction are never satisfied and neither are human eyes." *(Proverbs 27:19-20 NIV)*

"My advice to you is for you to get eyes that can see, ears that can hear, then turn and I will heal you. That is what one of my prophets said of my Son Jesus Christ. He said,

"Go and tell this people: Be ever hearing, but never understanding; be ever seeing, but never perceiving.' Make the heart of this people calloused; make their ears dull and close their eyes. Otherwise they might see with their eyes, hear with their ears, understand with their hearts, and turn and be healed." *(Isaiah 6:9-10 NIV)*

"And that is exactly what my Son Jesus Christ did when he came into the world.

"Jesus said, 'For judgment I have come into this world, so that the blind will see and those who see will become blind. Some of the Pharisees who were with Him heard Him say this and asked, What? Are we blind too? Jesus said, If you were blind, you would not be guilty of sin but now that you claim you can see, your guilt remains." *(John 9:39-41 NIV)*

"That goes for all of you! Now that you claim a God does exist even though you say I don't your guilt remains! But if you would take it upon yourself to blind your eyes from everything you see, and deafen your ears to everything you hear in this wicked dying world you live in, and refocus your eyes and ears on Me, the Lord your God, and turn to Me, then I would heal you. That is the exact reason my Son Jesus Christ appeared on this earth: to destroy Satan's darkness that plagues the hearts, souls, and minds of *my people.*"

"The one who does what is sinful is of the devil, because the devil has been sinning from the beginning. **THE REASON** *the Son of God appeared was to destroy the devil's work."* (1 John 3:8 NIV)

"Let me tell you the main reason why you rebel against me, the Lord your God! The reason is: the minute you see the word sin you relate it to your lifestyles of living. You enjoy doing what you want, how you want, and whatever you want, whether it's according to my word or not. That goes for you believers of mine too. What? Yes, you too! But of course that was why I sent my Spirit into the world. I had to in order for me to continue my work in your lives."

"When I was on the cross I spoke the words, "IT IS FINISHED!" What was finished? Your redemption of forgiveness from Me to you in order for you to get into heaven with Me in My glory. The reason I left was so I could finish My work in you through My Holy Spirit."

"That is the process where many of you *my people* have a problem with Me, even My so called followers, and believers of mine! You won't allow me to finish my work I began in you when I saved you."

"Why? Because YOU take my salvation for granted like you do your lives until it's too late. I told my disciples:

"But I tell you the truth: It is for your good I am going away. Unless I go away, the Counselor will not come to you but if I go, I will send Him to you. When he comes, he will convict the world in regard to sin and righteousness and judgment: in regard to sin, because men do not believe in me; in regard to righteousness, because I am going to the Father, where you can see me no longer, and in regard to judgement, because the prince of this world now stands condemned."

(John 16:7-11 NIV)

"I want you to notice what sin I am focused on when I say, 'the devil has been sinning from the beginning'. First of all, you weren't there in the beginning, but I was! I knew you before the foundations of the world were even laid. But you didn't exist! The devil did! You ought to read it in my word."

"Way before any of you were brought into existence, an angel in heaven who was with me said:

"I will ascend above the top of the clouds; I will make myself like the Most High."   *(Isaiah 14:14 NIV)*

"Guess who it was? The one who has been sinning from the beginning! That is why you read the words my Son Jesus Christ spoke:

"He replied, 'I saw Satan fall like lightning from heaven. I have given you authority to trample on snakes and scorpions AND TO OVERCOME ALL THE POWER of the enemy; nothing will harm you.'"

(Luke 10:18-19 NIV)

"But you don't know how to use that power in your lives for one simple reason, the biggest sin in your life! It is your ego within yourself that says, like Lucifer said, 'I will be like the Most High, and I will ascend to the top of the clouds.' I have a right to look down on people and judge them for their lifestyles of living in rebellion according to your word.'"

"You even persecute your own brothers and sisters who worship me in your gatherings, saying, 'You don't follow our belief, our doctrine, our faith and our customs. Thus you will not enter the kingdom of God as we will.'"

"As for the rest of you, you could not care less who I am to you as your creator. In other words: 'I do as I wish, and I will still get into heaven because God promised me eternal life, and God does not lie.' You're right! I don't lie! The devil does! So you would rather listen to Him, than listen to me.

"Jerusalem, Jerusalem, you who killed the prophets and stone those sent to you, how often I have longed to gather your children together, as a hen gathers her chicks under her wings, and you were not willing. Look, your house is left to you desolate. For I tell you, you will not see me again until you say, Blessed is he who comes in the name of the Lord." (Matthew 23:37-39 – Luke 13:34-35 NIV)

"That is why your house - your life - is left to you desolate, totally full of unhappiness and depressing uncertainty; totally lacking peace within itself because you cannot recognize why I came for you. I just told you a while ago why my Son appeared - to destroy the works of Satan! But now I say to you: you **WILL NOT** see me again until you say, 'Blessed is he who comes in the name of the Lord!'"

"The same goes for you, My body of Christ! That is why your churches are left to you desolate. That is why you will not see Me again until you say, 'Blessed is He who comes in the name of the Lord,' either in My second coming, or the day I call you home. You die on this earth! Hopefully by then you will have gotten rid of the most unforgiving sin under the heavens … totally ignoring Me and My word."

"That goes for you critical, judgmental Christians, too, who take it upon yourselves to sit on my throne and judge and condemn people to hell over their sins in their lives. Thus, you are totally blind to your own sin of acting like Satan who fell from heaven for his ego hearted attitude towards me, the Lord God of heaven and earth, saying, 'I will ascend above the clouds and be like the Most High!' I don't think you have the slightest idea what you have hanging over your own heads because of your attitudes towards my hurting and dying world you live in, <u>TRYING</u> to be like me, judging the world. I specifically told you,

"Do not judge, or you too will be judged. For in the same way you judge others, you will be judged, and with the measure you use, it will be measured to you.

(Matthew 7:1-2 NIV)

"There are different measures you use for people you judge in this world, depending on what sins they are committing. Sin is sin! If you want to see a sin, I am looking at one from my throne that you literally fail to see: it is the sin Lucifer committed in my presence that got Him booted out of heaven in the first place."

"He said, 'I will be like the Most High and ascend on top of the clouds!' Isn't that what you are symbolically saying, when you say, 'We are leaving in the clouds on Jesus Christ's return, a rapture, while the rest of this world is going to be judged by God for them not being like us?' If you are going to take it upon yourselves to justify your righteousness by creating a so-called rapture to escape my divine judgments on *my people* on earth after you leave, what should my judgment be on you upon your arrival in heaven, as you left everyone behind to receive my judgments since they weren't one of you?"

"The reason I ask that question is because according to your theory, those left behind are now going to be judged for not living for me the way they should have been living for me. Yet, you judged them the whole time you were on earth in the midst of all of them, before I came and got you in your 'rapture.'"

"Have you ever noticed what people do when they know they have guests coming over to their house? I'm sure you do it, too. When you have planned for guests to come over, or you get an unexpected phone call saying there is company coming over, you go on a cleaning spree. You go way out of your way to clean and organize your home to make the guests feel welcome. Do you not? Even if they are just relatives!"

"I am saying that you have this made-up mindset that I am coming for you unannounced through a 'rapture', and all of a sudden there is a disappearance of you followers of mine off the face of the earth you live in. Why? Because sin and the presence of evil is only going to gain strength in its power and force in the lives of those who are in rebellion towards me, the Lord your God! Yet, I do not see any effort on your part whatsoever in cleaning up your houses – your inner souls and churches - for me, the Lord your God! All I see are wicked spirits in you that want My wrath poured out on everyone around you...since they are not like you are."

"I told you, 'With the measure you use in judging *my people*, the same measure will be used for you.' So as you envision my long powerful arm pounding the earth through divine judgments on those left behind, likewise you will be pounded by the same powerful arm for being so judgmental. You won't be allowed into My kingdom of heaven for being unforgiving, merciless Pharisees and Sadducees with your faith, doctrine and religions."

"Then I heard a loud voice in heaven say: Now have come the salvation and the power and the kingdom of our God, and the authority of the Messiah. For the accuser of our brothers and sisters, who accuses them before our God day and night, has been hurled down." (Revelation 12:10 NIV)

"Remember, I saw Satan fall like lightning from heaven. Do you remember why he fell? He ascended above the clouds to be like me the Most High, while being an accuser of the brethren!"

"Do you know what you're doing when you see yourselves leaving this world through your teaching of a rapture? You're ascending yourselves above the clouds, trying to be like the Most High, putting words and passages of scripture interpretations of your own reasoning in my HOLY written word that are not there, only to top it off with being the accuser of the brethren. Then you condemn them to hell over their sins."

"The highway of the upright turns away and departs from evil; he who guards his way protects his life (soul). *Pride goes before destruction and a haughty spirit before a fall."*
(Proverbs 16:17-18 AMP)

"Thus, you have totally made yourselves enemies of the cross. How can you do that when it is written,

"They triumphed over Him by the blood of the Lamb and by the word of their testimony; they did not love their lives so much as to shrink from death.
(Revelation 12:11 NIV)

"In other words, you shouldn't fear death, since you are saved by My Son's blood, Who is the Lamb that was slain from the creation of the world, for the sins of the world. Wouldn't you consider yourselves a **SPECIAL** task force in the time of the anti-Christ's appearance in this world that I could use to <u>MY GLORY?</u>" says the Lord. "My Son, Jesus Christ, didn't only die for the sins of the world, but for My word He spoke unto the people. He had to die for My word He spoke in order for it to be HOLY and blameless before me, the Lord God of heaven and earth."

"My Son, Jesus Christ, wasn't anything like any of you. He didn't speak My word and live like a hypocrite! He didn't claim to love me and condemn everyone to hell. All He said was whoever doesn't listen to My word which I spoke would be condemned at the last day."

"That goes for everyone in all creation - saved or not! Just because you are saved doesn't mean you listen to My word. Even if you do, there is no obedience to it whatsoever. It is when you listen to My word, and then through obedience act on it while being saved that you are given eternal life."

"My Son died for those he loved! You? Forget it! You can't even die unto your own people who truly love you in your own personal life, your own family, much less for others and my written word. The only

54

written words of mine you die for are the passages of scripture that fulfill your selfish, self-centered spirit, which is evil in my presence."

"You come along with your own mind full of human reasoning, understanding, and interpretations of My word without any consultation, or any intercessory prayer to Me, the Lord your God, thus teaching *my people* deceptive lies they whole-heartedly believe. You have literally released a powerful spirit of witchcraft within My body of believers; one that is forever and ever going to affect millions of souls within My body in the coming days, if they don't come into the light of My word."

"Have you ever read,

"The light shines in the darkness, and the darkness has not overcome it."

(John 1:5 NIV)

"In this case it would mean there is no rapture, even though you have been claiming there is, which means very dark days are up the road for the body of Christ! But if you have My Son, Jesus Christ, in your hearts and souls where He belongs, He is the light that is going to shine in the darkness you are going to encounter."

"Seriously! Think this through! My Son, Jesus Christ, of all people that walked the face of the earth, would've gotten the privilege of a rapture in His life, if anyone! He never committed sin in his life, and loved everyone under the sun. He wasn't given a rapture as His way of escaping my judgment wrath on mankind. Instead, He encountered my wrath judgment on mankind Himself, rejected by every one of you as He was led away to His crucifixion and death on the cross."

"Even in the darkest hours of His life, He said,

"Father, forgive them, for they do not know what they are doing."

(Luke 23:34 NIV)

His light was still shining in the midst of the darkness: the rejection He got from all of you. The darkness even manifested itself in the eyes of the people there to see."

"From noon until three in the afternoon darkness came over the land."
(Matthew 27:45 – Mark 15:33 – Luke 23:44 NIV)

"His light still shined in the darkness all the way unto His death on the cross. After His resurrection days had passed, He was among His disciples teaching them all they were to do in their last commission here on this earth. Then He was taken up into heaven right before the disciples' eyes. You can call that His rapture, if you want, even though he didn't disappear! He was taken away in the clouds while his disciples watched."

"Out of pure love, He died according to His Father's will for you, His children. In other words, He had his date set of leaving this world like you do when you literally die, or I come, in my second coming! So, why do you take it upon yourselves to teach such a deceptive lie amidst yourselves of a rapture for you to escape my judgment on mankind, while thinking a group of mankind will be left behind to endure my judgments? Does that sound like what my Son did for you?"

"If He'd had the privilege of a rapture before my judgment on mankind, He would've disappeared and all of you would've had to die your own crucifixions to save your souls."

"Are you kidding? You think your sin-filled blood would've been given that privilege? You are sick-minded people to even come up with a notion of that sort. Only Satan would put that in your thoughts and minds. Repent of your ignorance you snakes! My Son, Jesus, died for mankind once and for all! By the same token, He will come back once and for all for all of mankind, ready, or not! That was why the apostles were told,

"This same Jesus, who has been taken from you into heaven, will come back in the same way you have seen Him go into heaven."   *(Acts 1:11 NIV)*

"The same way He died for you is the same way you die for Him. Take up your cross and follow Him! I thought you wanted to be like Him?"

"But God demonstrates his own Love for us in this: While we were still sinners, Christ died for us."   *(Romans 5:8 NIV)*

"But I guess not! You want to be better than Him to think you don't deserve anyone else's punishment on you. You want people to die to themselves and their ways before you show mercy, love and compassion. What do you think my hurting people are enduring because of your attitudes towards them and sin in this world?"

"This spirit of witchcraft you have released upon yourselves within my body of believers is going to be dealt with in a way you would never imagine in your life time. But, don't worry. I don't blame it all on you personally. It is My leaders who teach it, whether just some of it, or most of it. I hold my own people responsible for their own faiths and beliefs for this very simple reason:

"It is written: As surely as I live, says the Lord, every knee will bow before me; every tongue will acknowledge God. So then, each of us will give an account of ourselves to God."   *(Romans 14:11-12 NIV)*

"For the Son of Man is going to come in his Father's glory with his angels, and then he will reward each person according to what they have done."   *(Matthew 16:27 NIV)*

"Do you see what you just read? When my Son comes with His angels He is going to hand out rewards. Unlike your teaching that you all disappear who believe in Me while all those that don't believe in Me stay behind to face the end of times. Do you see yourselves getting rewards in your rapture, while the rest get theirs in my second coming? Does that really make sense to you?"

"In your teaching quest, you have set a standard within my body of so-called believers who are waiting for the return of my Son in a magical form of disappearance! Why? Don't you remember what Jesus answered the chief priests and teachers of the law when they asked Him, "Are you, the Son of God?" Mind you, He was on trial for you and your sins. He answered,

"You have said so, Jesus replied. But I say to all of you: From now on you will see the Son of Man sitting at the right hand of the Mighty One and coming on the clouds of heaven."   *(Matthew 26:64 – Mark 14:62 – Luke 22:69 NIV)*

'In others words, Jesus Christ was about to be glorified in the darkest hours of His life, by obtaining His reign and sitting at the right hand of God, and then being seen in the future coming in the clouds of heaven for His people. Do you realize what you have created over the years within your own body of believers? You have created a peaceful atmosphere of being in, what I call, 'self-denial'," says the Lord! "In other words, end time events are not even an issue to you as my body of believers since you won't be here according to your teachings and beliefs."

"When people are saying, Peace and safety, destruction will come on them suddenly, as labor pains on a pregnant woman, and they WILL NOT escape."
    (1 Thessalonians 5:3 NIV)

"The approach you have to this passage of scripture in my word is used towards the anti-Christ that is coming into the world in the near future. Why? Because that is how he is going to deceive the nations in convincing them he is the savior of the world who has finally established world peace."

"He will be a master of deception and will become arrogant; he will destroy many without warning. He will even take on the Prince of princes in battle, but he will be broken, though not by human power."   *(Daniel 8:25 NLT)*

"In case no one has ever told you, as a leader or leaders of *my people,* by telling them of a rapture that doesn't even exist, you are doing what the anti-Christ will do when he gets here. You have even made millions of dollars from the teachings with which you have deceived *my people,* because you told them what their itching ears like to hear. You have created a deceptively peaceful atmosphere in the midst of world chaos that is going to be right in your faces."

My Son Himself said, '*When these things begin to take place, stand up and lift up your heads, because your redemption is drawing near.*'"

(Luke 21:28NIV)

"But no! You leaders have convinced *my people* to just go on about life. Jesus has got your back! Your deception and arrogance will be your downfall along with the many innocent followers of yours who believe your deceptive words."

"All this comes by way of you entering through the north gate of the temple, the highest point of the temple, where my Son's head lays on the cross. Actually, if you are going to choose to come in by the north gate, where my Son's head lays, then you should experience a renewing of your mind within yourself!"

Your mind should be renewed, if nothing else, through the piercing of the crown of thorns upon his head that was beating with brute force, piercing Him in the temple. But you don't! All you experience is an arrogant spirit that thinks no one can change its ways of thinking, and reasoning. Especially when it comes to your faith and religions!"

"I looked, and I saw a figure like that of a man. From what appeared to be his waist down he was like fire, and from there up his appearance was as bright as glowing metal. He stretched out what looked like a hand and took me by the hair of my head. The Spirit lifted me up between earth and heaven and in the visions of God he took me to Jerusalem, to the entrance of the north gate of the inner court, where the idol that provokes to jealousy stood. And there before me was the

glory of the God of Israel, as in the vision I had seen in the plain. Then he said to me, Son of man, look toward the north. So I looked, and in the entrance north of the gate of the altar I saw this idol of jealousy."   *(Ezekiel 8:2-5 NIV)*

"As many of you claim to have knowledge of me, that idol of jealousy sits in the inner most part of the temple you are seeing. I'm not speaking of jealousy out in the world as you know it! People being jealous over material things others have they don't, and women jealous about other women!"

"Ministers are jealous about other ministers! Really? Yes, really! And they supposedly serve the same God! I am speaking of the jealousy found within my own body of Christ: Believers! Especially so called leaders in your body of believers! They are trying to out-do each other in reaching souls; out-perform each other, out-dress each other, shoving religious names onto my people like a lottery pick of numbers to see if you can win the big one. They are jealous about having the best looking building compared to others; jealous of the anointing one has on their life compared to yours… that's if you even have one!"

"But the biggest jealousy I see amidst my people is the jealousy you have towards people being wicked in the world you live in. What? Yes, jealous over their prosperity of injustice, or riches in scamming others. Jealousy of their sexual freedom they enjoy, while you have to remain pure in my presence," says the Lord! "Jealous they can say, and speak their minds while you must stay calm and quiet while turning the other cheek! Need I go on with examples of jealousy?"

"Why are you jealous of wicked people prospering, while you suffer over righteousness? It's simple: you are not living for Me, the Lord your God, but for yourself! Is that simple enough? You are like the son who stayed home with his father the whole time, while the brother left with his wealth and squandered every bit of it on prostitutes and whores while living a wild life style. The prodigal son! So you say to me, 'I have been with you this whole time, and you never gave me a special dinner consisting of a fattened calf to celebrate.'"

"I just look at you with tears in my eyes and say, I gave you my Son! Your egotistic sins cost my Son His life. But your wickedness of knowledge, and your own reasoning within your own hearts, and minds pierced his mind with the crown of thorns that was smashed and beat upon His head. I allowed it for only <u>ONE</u> reason: for you to renew your minds towards Me, the Lord your God through my Son, Jesus Christ!"

"Since, then, you have been raised with Christ, set your hearts on things above, **WHERE CHRIST IS***, seated at the right hand of God. Set your minds on things above, not on earthly things. For you died, and your life is now hidden with Christ in God. When Christ, who is your life, appears, then you will also appear with Him in glory."* *(Colossians 3:1-4 NIV)*

"You do realize that when He appears, you will be with Him? You will either be caught up in the clouds, since you are still here on earth for His return, or in the clouds with Him, since you were already with Him in glory after you died in this life to the next."

"Enoch, the seventh from Adam, prophesied about them: See, the Lord is coming with thousands upon thousands of his Holy ones." *(Jude 1:14 NIV)*

"There is nothing in relation to a disappearance off the face of the earth in what you just read! I pointed this out because this is one of my <u>BIGGEST,</u> heartbreaking sorrows I Am dealing with before my return," says the Lord! "That was why I showed my prophet Ezekiel what I did!"

"He brought me into the inner court of the house of the Lord, and there at the entrance to the temple, between the portico and the altar, were about twenty five men. With their backs toward the temple of the Lord and their faces towards the east, they were bowing down to the sun in the east." *(Ezekiel 8:16 NIV)*

"Though twenty five is a small number, it symbolically represents you people of mine who are in my temple, Jesus Christ, by way of the north gate. You live in a world plagued by darkness that would represent night. So you turn your backs on my temple, Jesus Christ, while within your own temples, your own lives, you wait on the sun in the east to rise in your darkened world."

"My Son is the light of the world! You are supposed to be the light of the world! So why do you turn your backs on my Son through self-denial of dealing with the issues of darkness?"

"He said to me, 'Have you seen this, son of man? Is it a trivial matter for the people of Judah to do the detestable things they are doing here? Must they also filled the land violence and continually arouse my anger? Look at them putting the branch to their nose! Therefore I will deal with them in anger; I will not look on them with pity or spare them. Although they shout in my ears, I will not listen to them.'"
(Ezekiel 8:17 NIV)

"Not only have you deceived millions of my believers, but your anticipation of my return has nothing more in it than you awaiting judgments against all those you consider your enemies in this life you live. That is why Satan has succeeded in his quest of deceiving all of you through pride and arrogance."

"But many who are first will be last, and many who are last will be first."
(Matthew 19:30 – Mark 10:31- Luke 13:30 NIV)

"When I say people are saying peace and safety, sudden destruction comes like labor pains on a pregnant woman, I know you impulsively remember my Son teaching his disciples about grief. He said,

"A woman giving birth to a child has pain because her time has come but when her baby is born she forgets the anguish because of her joy that a child is born into the world."
(John 16:21 NIV)

"So, you use it in reference to a struggling, heartache situation one goes through as encouragement to help them get through their sorrow and anguish in helping them find comfort, peace and happiness about their circumstance and situation. You tell them, 'These are like birth pains in a woman's life that is pregnant and ready to bring forth a new life. That's what all this is, Baby! Hang in there! That's great! God's bringing forth new life in you, hang in there! God's doing a new thing for you!'"

"And, so it is! I am trying to give you a new thing, my child, a new thing pertaining to the very near future! Birth pains that my Son told you about before His return: days of great tribulation never seen since the world began, and never to be equaled again. If those days had not been cut short no one would survive."

*"But, for the sake of the **ELECT**, those days will be cut short."*

(Matthew 24:21-22 NET)

"I am trying to stop all of you supposedly wise people from coming into my Kingdom through the north gate of my temple with your own mental and psychological reasoning, understanding, and interpretations of My word. You go to all your cemetery classes - I'm sorry - seminary classes, only to be taught of men!"

"All you have done is become a deceptive tool of Satan unto *my people* through your own teachings of knowledge and understanding. That is how you came up with so many names of faiths, religions and denominations that people can rely on, unto the salvation of their soul. You have found many ways of salvation with which one can get into heaven…even a rapture! However, I only gave you one way to God your Father! Did you forget it?"

"Thomas said to Him, Lord, we don't know where you are going, so how can we know the way? Jesus answered, I am the way and the truth and the life. No one comes to the Father except through me.   *(John 14:5-6 NIV)*

If My Son, Jesus Christ, is the way, the truth, and the life and no one comes to Me, the Father, except through Him - how in the hell can a magical disappearance of people off the face of the earth replace a second coming of my Son, Jesus Christ? Jesus Christ is,

"...the stone you builders rejected, which has become the cornerstone. Salvation is found in no one else, for there is no other name under heaven given to mankind by which we must be saved." (Acts 4:11-12 NIV)

"I don't get it, Lord! He is coming in the clouds, isn't He?"

"Yes, He is, and **EVERY** eye is going to see Him.

"Look, he is coming with the clouds, and EVERY EYE will see Him, even those who pierced Him , and all the peoples of the earth will mourn because of Him. So shall it be! Amen!" (Revelation 1:7 NIV)

"But you have come up with this notion of Jesus' coming to be something that cannot be seen with the natural eyes, only spiritual eyes. So, why would the nations of the earth wail and mourn if they won't see it? Actually, this isn't even a debate about my coming, anyway. It is more of a message to you about how you have literally become enemies of the cross my Son endured, scorning its shame for your salvation of your eternal life. And now you have no shame whatsoever in how you present yourselves to me, God your Father in heaven."

"Let me assure you, my words will come to pass right before your very eyes, and every eye will see it.

"This is what the Lord said to me: Go and buy a linen belt and put it around your waist, but do not let it touch water. So I bought a belt, as the Lord directed, and I put it around my waist. Then the word of the Lord came to me a second time: Take the belt you bought and are wearing around your waist, and go now to Perath and hide it there in the crevice of the rocks. So I went and hid it at Perath, as the Lord told me. Many days later the Lord said to me, Go now to Perath and get the belt I told you to hide there. So I went to Perath and dug up the belt and took it from the place where I had hidden it, but now it was ruined and completely useless. Then the word of the Lord came to me: This is what the Lord

says: In the same way I will ruin the pride of Judah and the great pride of Jerusalem. These wicked people, who refuse to listen to my words, who follow the stubbornness of their hearts and go after other gods to serve and worship them, will be like this belt – completely useless! For as a belt is bound around a man's waist, so I bound the house of Israel and the whole house of Judah to me, declares the Lord, to be my people for my renown and praise and honor. But they have not listened."   *(Jeremiah 13:1-11 NIV)*

"I will ruin the pride of the church and My people," says the Lord! "For you have taken my word and hid it in the crevices of your supposed, man-made, cement rock-heart foundations of churches of religions, faiths and denominations. This hides the true meaning of My word while watering it down to your preference in how things should be, and are going to be."

"All of you who search your own ways are completely useless to Me," says the Lord! "You go after your own gods while serving them, and worshipping them. Yet you refuse to listen to my words in their entirety by doing what you want, and believing only what you want to believe out of the stubbornness of your hard hearted hearts!"

"For the time will come when people will not listen to the true teaching. But people will find more and more teachers who please them. They will find teachers who say what they want to hear. People will stop listening to the truth. They will begin to follow the teaching in false stories.   *(2 Timothy 4:3-4 ERV)*

"That time is now! This only happened because you have chosen to come into my temple through highest point of the temple. The North Gate! If you want wisdom it can be given to you of me," says the Lord! "I promised it to you!"

*"If any of you lacks wisdom, you should ask of God, who gives generously to all **without** finding fault, and it will be given to you."*   *(James 1:5 NIV)*

"Do you see what you just read? I want you to learn of Me," says the Lord! "I don't hold anything against you, as this world does. My Son died for you in order for you to be forgiven of me, the Lord your God! We can start there in your search for wisdom of me," says the Lord. "How?"

"The fear of the Lord is the beginning of wisdom, and knowledge of the Holy One is understanding." (Proverbs 9:10 NIV)

"The fear I look for in *my people* is not a fear that traumatizes one's being over an encounter of the unknown, like millions of you fear death! The fear I speak of, is a fear that shows respect and honor towards Me, the Lord your God. It is a fear based on respect, like those who fear the laws of the land. They are not afraid of the law or the laws of the land, they just respect it while honoring it, saving themselves a lot of unnecessary regret. That should be the beginning of your wisdom. Respect me, and honor me with your lives," says the Lord. "Repent of your delusional mindsets and beliefs. You won't regret it! Stop trying to come in by the north gate! Therefore, whoever humbles themselves will be exalted! But whoever exalts themselves will be humbled!"

Chapter 5 - East and West Gates

"I say to you that many will come from the east and the west, and will take their places at the feast with Abraham, Isaac and Jacob in the kingdom of heaven. But the subjects of the kingdom will be thrown outside, into the darkness, where there will be weeping and gnashing of teeth." (Matthew 8:11-12 NIV)

During the vision of the temple given to me by God, I intently looked at the east and west gates where millions of souls were coming into the kingdom of heaven. As I looked at the compass I went into a trance, so to speak, as I looked at the pierced hands of my Lord and Savior, Jesus Christ. I was then overcome with an uncontrollable sorrow as I began to weep and wail from within my soul. From the heartfelt mindset I had, I knew it was out of compassion and broken heartedness that I was weeping uncontrollably over our Lord and Savior, Jesus Christ.

It was as when one finally accepts the true fact and reality of the loss of a loved one after that person passes away. The deeply embedded sorrow from within wouldn't stop coming out of me. My sorrow drained my physical strength, and I found myself lying on the floor of my cabin. I prayed earnestly unto the Lord God, my Father, saying, "I am so sorry for what we did, and have done to your Son, our Lord and Savior, Jesus Christ! Please forgive us, Father God, for our transgressions!"

As soon as the words came out of my mouth, a surge of peace came into my soul and spirit. The sorrowful pain left, but the tears kept coming as I kept looking at the nail pierced hands of our Lord and Savior, Jesus Christ. Then God the Father spoke!

He said, "Did you not realize it is not you crying over anything you are seeing? Rather it is I, the Lord God, your Father in heaven crying in you, and through you, over what is being done unto my Son, Jesus Christ, as of this very day. And I did say IS BEING DONE unto my Son, this very day and hour you are living in. You saw what they did to Him in the vision given to you of me, after he died for the sins of the world. But now I want you to see what I see in what they are doing to my Son now in this day and age," says the Lord!

"I will reveal it to you in order for you to tell *my people* of their wickedness that is before my face. It is the face of hypocrisy that is far worse than the faces of hypocrisy you give to each other in the lives you live amidst one another. If you have a right as humans to deal with each other's hypocrisy the way you do, how then shall I deal with yours?" says the Lord. "The first time my Son was crucified, He said, 'Father forgive them, for they know not what they do!'"

"But, now, in the days of Love, mercy and grace, you do know what you are doing. It would be like my Son saying on the cross, 'Father, forgive them, even though they know what they are doing!' Wretched cowards! You really think I would allow it that way in my presence," says the Lord, "that my Son would do that for you after what he already did for you? So as it is, you are bringing my word to pass in your very own personal lives,

"If we deliberately keep on sinning after we have received the knowledge of the truth, no sacrifice for sins is left, but only a fearful expectation of judgment and of raging fire that will consume the enemies of God. Anyone who rejected the law of Moses died without mercy on the testimony of two or three witnesses. How much more severely do you think a man deserves to be punished who has trampled the Son of God under foot ; who has treated as an unholy thing the blood of the covenant that sanctified Him, and who has insulted the Spirit of grace? For we know Him who said, It is mine to avenge ; I will repay, and again, The Lord

will judge his people. It is a dreadful thing to fall into the hands of the Living God." *(Hebrews 10:26-31 NIV)*

"As I said, many will come from the east and the west to take their place in the kingdom. You know why? If you take a good look at the compass, and what lies on the east and west gate points of the compass, you will see my Son's arms of Love and forgiveness open wide unto a world full of hate and unforgiveness, a world full of addictions of all types and forms of lust and pleasure. Pride, arrogance, and evil hearts that want more for themselves than others."

"That is why millions of *my people* will come in through the east and west gates of the temple that represent unconditional love! That's the easiest love one can live by: No commitment involved, do as you please, go and come as you want, and you are still loved. It was unconditional when I gave it to win you back unto myself," says the Lord.

"It was my way of showing you true heavenly love that would not, and will not, hold anything against you that may have happened in your life before having a relationship with me, your Heavenly Father!"

"Before my Son came, we couldn't have an intimate relationship between the two of us, because of my Holiness, and the sins in your life. So I took it upon myself to come to you as the Son, to offer myself for you through love, mercy, grace and forgiveness. And you accepted it, or you believe in it. You do that to each other in the lives you live! Do you not? You meet someone who all of a sudden is special to you. You go out and spend time together to get to know each other better to build a bond between the two of you that will hopefully turn into love. Actually, love already lives in you! You just want to find someone to share it."

"I don't know if you have ever noticed when you are dating and seeing each other how just about everything around you is unconditional love. Why? Because that's how bad you want them to get close to you, and notice that you love them. Once love starts filling the air, the bonding begins to take place and conditions begin to change. They change so much, you end up going to the altar, giving your lives to each other and exchanging vows, even if you are of the same sex as the other one you are going to marry."

"Once married, everything changes between the two of you as far as commitment and devotion goes. Unconditional love then turns into supposed total commitment and devotional love towards each other. Or at least it should!"

"That is why you young girls who give your bodies away to satisfy the pervert you're with never get the respect you deserve. Your insecurity in your own life gives away to his demand of pleasure, rather than love. You really think you can win him over with your body, when it is your heart you should be exposing - not your flesh."

"Read my lips! Sex has nothing to do with love! That is called lust! So when you get married, unconditional love is out of the question. That's even if they marry you! Either you are their slave, or they are yours in the relationship. It turns into mediocre commitment and love."

"Then your spouse cheats on you and breaks your heart and trust; yet, you hold onto them, giving them a sense of unconditional love, though you are broken and shattered within your own being. I guess you think that's how I will accept your unrepentant hearts, through my Son's love He gave to you that literally cost Him his life."

"That is why divorce rules the world you live in, even in your so called realm of Christianity. So! If you can file for a divorce over unfaithfulness, can I not do the same to you?" says the Lord. "Did you say, 'No'? Why? Because I am God? All of you know I hate divorce! You didn't? Read it!"

"I hate divorce, says the Lord God of Israel, and I hate a man's covering Himself with violence as well as his garment, says the Lord Almighty. So guard yourself in your spirit, and do not break faith."   *(Malachi 2:16 NIV)*

'Lord! I was as faithful as I knew how to be and I still got cheated on! My heart got broken, and even with forgiveness in my heart I knew it would never be the same. So are you going to be angry at me over a divorce I went through Lord? I already hurt over the divorce itself and the broken heartedness that comes with it and now to have it on my conscience knowing you hate divorce, God?"

"Oh! Listen to yourself justifying your actions you took over a situation you had no control over," says the Lord! "So! What if I told you that I, the Lord your God did have control over what I sent (my Son) into your life to help you with -- your broken heartedness. But you sent Him away with a written certificate of divorce. Why, because He was unfaithful to you? Since you suffered over something someone did to you, and He didn't intervene? He didn't heal a loved one of yours? He didn't bring back your unfaithful spouse, even though you had a heart of forgiveness to try and work things out?"

"You claim to love Him, my Son, and have Him as your Lord and Savior. Yet you can't do what he did for you as his son or daughter, can you? Even as my body of believers! As it is written,

"Now as the church submits to Christ, so also wives should submit to their husbands in **EVERYTHING.** *Husbands love your wives, just as Christ loved the church and gave Himself up for her, to make her holy, cleansing her by the washing with water through the word."*   *(Ephesians 5:24-26 NIV)*

"No one knows how to devote themselves to those basic rules of life anymore, much less to my word," says the Lord, "the word that became flesh, My Son, Jesus Christ! (John 1:14) Why, because I am such a loving and merciful God who forgives everything and everyone under the sun? Well guess what? I do, to make you pure and holy in my presence. But you don't want it that way. You want it your way - of being forgiven and accepted as you are in your wicked, selfish ways."

"You might get that from the one you are married to, or in love with. Some of you even go as far as sharing yourself with all the other men or women they are cheating with because of their unfaithfulness. Your insecurity in life fearing the unknown makes you accept their unfaithfulness as a way of life. So you sleep with them, and the next day they are with someone else. They come back and act as though nothing happened because you love them that much."

"That's what millions of my followers do with their religions! They worship it, then worship me! You can be like that to each other if you so prefer but ME! You can forget that! I love my Son more than any of you I have ever created. He came to me Himself with a prayer petition to let the hour of suffering pass by Him. Do you recall that in his life? Probably not!"

"He withdrew about a stone's throw beyond them, knelt down and prayed. Father, if you are willing, take this cup from me; yet not my will, but yours be done." (Luke 22:41-42 NIV)

'Do you know what he was praying about? The suffering he was about to endure on your behalf, because of all the rebellion and sin in your life! Did I answer his request? You think I would have! If anybody deserved an answer to a prayer, it would've been Him. But I didn't! That was the **ONLY** way I found it in my heart to accept you into my kingdom: Jesus Christ, my Son! So what did he get instead of an answer to his prayer? If you read my word like you should, you would know the answer.

"An angel appeared from heaven to Him and strengthened Him."

(Luke 22:43 NIV)

"The only angels that have appeared to you are deceptive lying angels empowered by wicked spirits straight from the pit of hell. Why?

Because you <u>DO NOT</u> want to let go of your selfish perverted ways," says the Lord! "That is why you have no strength in you over your circumstances and situations in your lives. That is why millions will perish into outer darkness, where there will be weeping and gnashing of teeth. Because you hold on to the unconditional love you found at the cross where my Son was hung for your sins, without giving me your total commitment of your life, soul and being," says the Lord.

"So if you think I am going to be like you, who put up with unfaithful, perverted partners, abusive partners, who beat you black and blue and insult you while downgrading you, mentally torturing you, and yet you keep taking them back because you say you love them, you had better think again. Unconditional love is one thing, but to degrade yourself where you get no respect or honor is another."

"My Son's unconditional love cost Him his life. He laid it down once and for all like you did when you gave yourself over to your husband, wife, boyfriend, or girlfriend, or even your children. You really think I am going to allow you to disrespect my Son like you do each other as humans? That was why the angel appeared to Him in the time of his anguish and sincere, sorrowful prayer: to strengthen Him!"

"And being in anguish, he prayed more earnestly, and sweat was like drops of blood falling to the ground."   *(Luke 22:44 NIV)*

'Ha! You can't even find time in your selfish lives to even give me a thank you praise for letting you live another day in your self-centered life," says the Lord! "That was why my Son came to his disciples and found them in the condition they were in, just like a lot of you are."

*"When he rose from prayer and went back to his disciples, **HE FOUND THEM ASLEEP**, exhausted from sorrow."*   *(Luke 22:45 NIV)*

"This life has exhausted all of you where it has literally put you to sleep. So he asked them what I am about to ask you!

"Why are you sleeping? He asked them, Get up and pray so that you will not fall into temptation."   *(Luke 22:46 NIV)*

"That was why my Son rose on the third day! Only to take His life back up in the power of the Spirit of the Father! In the power of my Spirit," says the Lord! "To empower each of you that decides to whole heartedly give yourselves to my will in your life being done on earth as it is in heaven."

"That is where you fail miserably in your relationship with abusers. You did the right thing in laying down your life for the other because you were ready to share your life with another. But you didn't take it back up in the power of my Spirit you believe in so much when you realized your married life became a nightmare from hell. You very well know God made man for woman, and woman for man! So what did you do when you realized your lover became your pimp? When you realized you married a sexual addict who never is satisfied, with lust living inside Him, or her; or you realized you married a shopaholic who spends money you don't even have which has you in debt with nothing to show for it?"

"You even take it upon yourself to challenge my established word that says God created man for woman, and woman for man! Why do you choose a partner you have no business with, though you are miserable as hell? But instead of taking your life back up in the ONLY name I gave you power to do it in, you are trying to take it back up in their name - whoever the hell they are!"

"What? Yes, whoever the hell they are! It is hell inside of them who wants to control you like it does all *my people* who believe in me. Your partner says they love you, yet they live for themselves more than they do you. It's their way, or no way! It's what they desire, not you. What they say goes, your opinion or input doesn't count, or matter! And some of you literally enslave yourselves to that possessive spirit in your life because of insecurity issues: it is the fear of the unknown."

"Just like millions do to me, the Lord their God, through their mediocre faith. They believe in me, yet live their lives apart from me," says the Lord! "That is why millions take their places in the kingdom of the Father in heaven not realizing they took my Son's unconditional love for granted. But as I mentioned in my word, *'...but the subjects of the kingdom will be thrown outside where there will be weeping and gnashing of teeth."* (Matthew 8:12 NIV)

"Guess you want to know who, or what, the subjects of the kingdom are? Let me try and explain it to you at a level and in a language you will understand. Some of you will disagree! But hear me out," says the Lord.

"Ask me if I care! This isn't about you, anyway! It's about my Son, Jesus Christ! Every one of you has been to school at one time or another in your life right? Some of you are still in school even after you graduate from grade school, right? For what? To study, or major in a class to earn a degree of education and knowledge in whatever you are being taught right?"

"Ok! Where are we going with this? When you attend school to be educated, you have what they call classes, with different subjects. That is the whole purpose of attending school, right, to be educated in different subjects. Now whether you failed them, or passed them is on you, yet you were taught those subjects. And whether they taught you right, or not is for you to discern. That's an issue that doesn't even exist in what my Son, taught you about me the Father! Why?"

"The chief priests and the whole Sanhedrin were looking for evidence against Jesus so that they could put Him to death, but they did not find any. Many testified falsely against Him, but their statements did not agree." (Mark 14:55-56 NIV)

'When I, God the Father, came to earth in the form of my Son I taught on many subjects of the kingdom. And just like it is in the education system of your world, all the subjects discussed and taught go hand in hand in order for you to pass from one grade to another, to help you get by in the life you live that requires reading, writing and arithmetic."

"So it is with you passing from this world you live unto my kingdom in heaven that is within you. Most of you think reaching my kingdom won't take place until you die in this world. No! My kingdom is within you! (Luke 17:20) You should let it start operating out of you from within."

"You come to me in the name of forgiveness to get into my kingdom of heaven since you passed your test in understanding why I forgive you. Yet you never accepted the subject of repentance. You failed miserably out of your own selfish perverted ways. You come to me for forgiveness since you understood my love for you in order to get into heaven. Yet you hate your brother and sister with a very bitter filled heart of un-forgiveness. Since they commit sins, you condemn them to hell for them."

"You come to me in my love, yet you can't even fathom loving a brother or a sister in me who is a different skin color than you are. You're racist, and prejudiced! Oh yeah, I see how you greet each other in your church services at the opening of a service. I see all the different nationalities and races in your gatherings. Unification like none other! You shake hands and hug each other just smiling away as though you looked forward to seeing each other in your church gatherings."

"Yet you don't fool me, you snakes," says the Lord! "What the hell is wrong with you people? You can literally see my Son nailed hand and foot to the cross, covered in blood that splattered itself all over every one of you, as the scriptures testify, "He will sprinkle the nations with his blood.""

"Not only are you ignorant in your warped-mindedness, but you even have religion clothing you are wearing as you approach the cross my

Son was hung on to die in the very shameful way He did for all of you, that in His name you would bow down. But you don't! Don't you remember anything He shared with you before He was crucified for your blind eyes to see, and deaf ears to hear?"

*"Jesus spoke to them again in parables, saying: The kingdom of heaven is like a king who prepared a wedding banquet for **HIS SON**. He sent his servants to those who had been invited to the banquet to tell them to come, but they refused to come. Then he sent some more servants and said, Tell those who have been invited that I have prepared my dinner: My oxen and fattened cattle have been butchered, and everything is ready. Come to the wedding banquet. But they paid no attention and went off – one to his field, another to his business. The rest seized his servants, mistreated them and killed them. The king was enraged. He sent his army and destroyed those murderers and burned their city. Then he said to his servants, The wedding banquet is ready, but those I invited did not deserve to come. So go to the streets corners and invite to the banquet anyone you find. So the servants went out into the streets and gathered all the people they could find, the bad as well as the good, and the wedding hall was filled with guests. But when the king came in to see the guests, he noticed a man there who was not wearing wedding clothes. Friend, he asked, How did you get in here without wedding clothes? The man was speechless. Then the king told the attendants, tie Him hand and foot, and throw Him outside, into the darkness, where there will be weeping and gnashing of teeth. For many are invited, but few are chosen."*

(Matthew 22:1-14 NIV)

"Let me start with the wedding clothes! At one time in the life you live it was intended for the woman to be married to wear a white dress that represented purity."

"Are you kidding Lord?"

"No, I AM not! You think I am because of the degraded society you live in. If you were familiar with my word, that you should spend more time reading, you would understand my point in saying that. My Son, Jesus Christ, is referred to as the bridegroom. You didn't know that did you? Look:

"Then I heard what sounded like a great multitude, like the roar of rushing waters and like peals of thunder, shouting: Hallelujah! For our Lord God Almighty reigns. Let us rejoice and be glad and give Him glory! For the wedding of the Lamb has come, and his bride has made herself ready. Fine linen, bright and clean, was given to her to wear." (Revelation 19:6-8 NIV)

"So there is a wedding gathering that is going to take place in the very near future for the Lamb of God, My Son Jesus Christ! He is the Lamb of God!"

"The next day John saw Jesus coming toward Him and said, Look, the Lamb of God, who takes away the sin of the world!" (John 1:29 NIV)

"This Lamb of God, my Son, Jesus Christ, we are talking about was slain before the foundations of the world were even laid."

"But with the precious blood of Christ, a lamb without blemish or defect. He was chosen before the creation of the world, but was revealed in these last times for your sake." (1 Peter 1:19-20 NIV)

"So this is what I want you to see in what I am saying to you in that parable you just read. The only way you will get to stay and attend the wedding of the Lamb - eternal life in heaven - is to be cleansed through His blood He shed on the cross to forgive you of your sins. The ONLY way you will even have a chance of attending the wedding of the Lamb is to do what the scripture said the bride did: **She got herself READY!** So because she made the effort in getting herself ready, a bright and fine clean linen was given to her to wear. That's what you should do as my believing child."

"I would say go to church, and make that your first priority in the life you live, but I won't! Why? What are they doing as my church in getting ready? They are waiting for me to come in the clouds while wishing and pronouncing impending judgments on everybody else on this earth who isn't part of them as though they are very important to me, and all others are not!"

"Yes, all evil is condemned by me," says the Lord, "<u>NOT MY PEOPLE!</u> So that goes for evil condemning hearts you walk around with all the days of your lives you live while going to church."

"Since you are so faithful to me," says the Lord, "do you gossip about others? Do you covet your neighbor's goods? Do you give out false accusations against others? Do you watch perverted movies while you're alone, while no one else is around? Are you teaching my people my word as it should be taught? Or are you compromising with them to keep your numbers of attendance up in order to get more money in your offerings?"

"My Son never took up money, and all He taught was about me, God, your Father, in heaven. The only offering He took up was **HIS LIFE!** Something the majority of you have miserably failed in - even so-called Christians! Need I go on? If you think you can do those things you do while others are not around, then you really haven't had a personal encounter with me yet," says the Lord.

"I am not looking for you to be perfect," says the Lord. "It's the notion that these things you do while no one else is around has you so naïve of me, and my true presence in your life. Though I am Spirit," says the Lord, "and cannot be seen, I am very well alive in your life...and you think I am not!"

"In others words, you tend to compare me to everyone else in this world who doesn't see what you do when you're alone. I am, right there with you! That is the meaning of the saying,

"I will never leave, nor fail you, nor forsake you."   (Deuteronomy 31:8)

But you want to keep forsaking your faith in me through your psychological mentality of being convinced you can fool me," says the Lord, "like you do everybody else."

"**<u>GO FOR IT!</u>** I am right there with you! I am not pinpointing anyone as a target with my message," says the Lord. "I love all my children I created for myself. I love every one of you! But there is only ONE for whom I opened the heavens."

"As soon as Jesus was baptized, he went up out of the water. At that moment heaven was opened, and he saw the Spirit of God descending like a dove and alighting on Him. And a voice from heaven said, This is my Son, whom I love; with Him I am well pleased." *(Matthew 3:16-17 NIV)*

"That was why He told you, '*No one comes to the Father, but through **ME!**'* So <u>LISTEN</u> to Him!'" *(Matthew 17:5 - Mark 9:7 - Luke 9:35)*

"ESPECIALLY YOU, my so-called body of Christ! In case no one's ever told you, the bride is also in reference to the body of Christ! Remember the parable of the ten virgins my Son Jesus Christ taught on? It was more directed at you my church, than anyone else:

"At that time the kingdom of heaven will be like ten virgins who took their lamps, and went out to meet the bridegroom. Five of them were foolish and five were wise. The foolish ones took their lamps, but did not take any oil with them. The wise, however, took oil in jars along with their lamps. The bridegroom was a long time in coming, and they all became drowsy and fell asleep. At midnight the cry rang out: Here's the bridegroom! Come out to meet Him! Then all the virgins woke up and trimmed their lamps. The foolish ones said to the wise, Give us some of your oil our lamps are going out. No, they replied, there may not be enough for the both of us. Instead, go to those who sell oil and buy some for yourselves. But while they were on their way to buy the oil, the bridegroom arrived. The virgins who were ready went in with Him to the wedding banquet. And the door was shut! Later the others also came, Sir! Sir! they said. Open the door for us! But he replied, I tell you the truth, I don't know you. Therefore keep watch, because you do not know the day nor the hour." *(Matthew 25:1-13 NIV)*

"Let me explain something to you that you need to start doing as followers of mine, whether you go to church, or not... As it is in your society you live in that says: if you don't go to church, you go to hell! But I say to you," says the Lord, "if you go to church, and don't change the ways of your hearts and attitudes towards me, the Lord your God in heaven, and my hurting and dying world, you will also go to hell!"

"Now let me clarify myself in what I AM saying to you," says the Lord. "The oil in my teaching represents my written word you hardly read, or even look into, since going to church is good enough for you. Those of you who don't go to church forget it when it comes to reading my word. But it is written for the both of you in my word,

"Your word is a lamp to my feet and a light for my path."
(Psalm 119:105 NIV)

"The lamp represents your life that should shine in the world of darkness in this life you live. But it doesn't work that way, does it? You can't even apply it to yourself in your own lives, much less for others. For the most of you it's because you take my word (the oil) for the lamp (your life) in portions that you apply to your lives, sort of like mixing oil with water! They don't mix too well, do they?"

"Water? Yes! Water! The watered-down sermons you give in your church gatherings. Your watered down hearts that drown the LOVE conviction you feel from me, the Lord your God, when you know you are wrong about being where you are, as opposed to where you are supposed to be. In other words, it's your way, or no way!"

"I guess that is why you take it upon yourselves to come in through the east and west gates of the temple, right? They represent my Son's loving arms spread wide for you out of his forgiveness towards you. Yet, you don't repent of your wicked, evil, perverted hearts full of lust, selfishness, unforgiveness, hatred, anger, prejudice, egotistic attitudes, pride, and arrogance. You are self-righteous people of religions, faiths, and denominations, not to mention your customs and rituals you present yourselves to me with."

"I told you, I am talking to you as my people, whether you live for me, or not; whether you go to church, or not! All of you know God said He is faithful to forgive you of your sins! God doesn't lie! No, I don't! So, if you are going to quote me at my promised word and accept it into your hearts and put it to work in your lives than do so in its entirety. Like this:

"If we confess our sins, he is faithful and just and will forgive us our sins and purify us from all unrighteousness."   *(1 John 1:9 NIV)*

"You tend to leave words out of my spoken word, only to justify your perverted hearts, and minds. I will forgive you of your sins AND purify you from all unrighteousness. But you can't be purified if you are not sincere in your watered down prayers for forgiveness you come at me with. So why bother explaining purification to you if you can't even repent with a true heart when you come unto me," says the Lord!

"Remember earlier in the message I said,

No one lights a lamp and puts it under a bowl?   *(Luke 8:16 NLT)*

"Well, your mediocre spirits and hearts towards me is a perfect example of one's attitude towards my unconditional love I gave unto all of you through my Son. In all honesty, do you really think I would contradict myself through my own word? You just read earlier,

'God is not a God of disorder, but of peace.'   *(1 Corinthians 14:33 NLT)*

'I AM the Prince of Peace!'"   *(Isaiah 9:6)*

"So be honest with yourself! If you are not at peace with yourself when you try to make me part of your life then something is wrong, and it's with you, not me! Why? Because you are constantly changing and being someone else, other than who you really are in me."

"I change not."   *(Malachi 3:6 NIV)*

"So if you want to take my forgiveness for granted, and live your lives to your own degraded, selfish pleasures, be my guest! But I WILL NOT subject my Son's suffering to your degraded mindset of thinking his death was the free token chip you can gamble with. Actually, His death and resurrection were willed by me, God the Father, to set my people free from the bondage of sin and selfish living. You see,

"Jesus replied, 'I tell you the truth, everyone who sins is a slave to sin. Now a slave has no permanent place in the family, but a son belongs to it forever. So if the Son sets you free, you will be free indeed.'"   *(John 8:34-36 NIV)*

"So, if you want to enter my kingdom of heaven through the east and west gates of my Son's love while you very well know you are a slave to your own pleasures and desires, go for it! But you have been now told a slave has no permanent place in the family. In others words, you can be part of my family who believes in God and claims to worship Him all the days of your life here on earth while carrying around all your little devils with you along your journey while my love and grace abounds. You just won't have a permanent place in my family when I demand your life from you, you hypocrite! My Son belongs to it forever so whom the Son sets free, is free indeed!"

"How do you feel when people accept your love for them, yet never acknowledge you for it? Mom? Dad? Grandpa? Grandma? You spread your arms of love wide for all those you hold close to you, yet you are never respected, or even noticed, especially in your old age! Nobody ever comes around to see you anymore! They don't call you just to talk or hear your voice. They put you in nursing homes! Well, it's because their lives demand so much it doesn't leave them time to do those things you are talking about."

"I agree one hundred percent! That's how all of you do me, too," says the Lord! "Hypocrites! You have no time in your busy lives for me," says the Lord! "Make time and efforts in your parent's lives before I call them home. If you don't, then you are left in total regret of not being there for them like you should've been. The same applies to me, the Lord your God! They put you in nursing homes where you will be taken care of out of the goodness and concern for you out of their hearts. Their intentions are good, yet you are lonely as hell in your old age."

"That comes from you taking me for granted and putting all your loved ones and family before me, the Lord your God. I could have defeated the loneliness in your life way before it even showed up; but, you took my love and forgiveness of your souls for granted that never allowed me to grow in you in helping you overcome all the adversity this life throws at you, my people."

"Why did I use that example? Because, that is how it will be for millions of you followers of mine in the time of the end, unless I am allowed to grow in you. Actually that goes for all of you in your society you live in. I just used those four relationship types in the lives you live, because I see them by the millions before me, crying their eyes out over their disrespectful children and grandchildren they have."

"Where did I go wrong, Lord," is all I hear! You didn't go wrong, they did! Just like millions of you will through your own deceptive, perverted ways of unrepentance, coming into my kingdom through the east and west gates of my extended loving arms of forgiveness and love for you."

"That goes for you church-going followers of mine, too! You came unto me, and accepted my open arms of love and forgiveness to you, yet you can't give it away freely like it was given to you. No! Like I told those of you with very intelligent, self-trained, educated, religious leaders you sit under who enter through the north gate of the temple through their own knowledge and wisdom. You eagerly await my second coming, so you can leave, and avoid my impending judgments against all those you spent your whole 'Christian life' condemning people to hell."

"That is why it is written in my word for you 'religious-righteous' thugs, and non-repentant children of mine!

"You diligently study the scriptures because you think that by them you possess eternal life. These are the scriptures that testify about me, yet you refuse to come to me to have life." (John 5:39-40 NIV)

"Sounds like discrimination to me, Lord!"

"Discrimination! I hold it against you because of who you are? Is that what you mean? If you knew who you are in me, you would not be who you are in yourself," says the Lord! "But since you want to throw up discrimination because you want to be who you are, and live as you are, and believe as you want, I will put that word discrimination between heaven and earth for all of you to see. Except, when you see it, it won't be the word **discrimination** you will see. It will be a symbol shaped like a cross: the cross of my Son, Jesus Christ! That's discrimination!"

"The same way you have treated what I gave every one of you out of my heart," says the Lord your God.

"He was oppressed and afflicted, yet he did not open his mouth; he was led like a lamb to the slaughter, and as a sheep before its shearer is silent, so he did open his mouth. By oppression and judgment he was taken away. Yet who of his generation protested? For he was cut off from the land of the living; for the transgression of my people he was punished. He was assigned a grave with the wicked, and with the rich in his death, though he did no violence, nor was any deceit in his mouth." (Isaiah 53:7-9 NIV)

"So, now, you have been shown the true discrimination that exists in the heavens between man and God. It has nothing to do with your hatred and racism issues you have on earth. It has nothing to do with your perverted ways of life, removing statues and everything that offends you because of race color, nationalities, and egos. What's your excuse for removing my Son out of your hearts? It has nothing to do with church and religion. It's the discrimination my Son got from all of you, for his LOVE, when he came to earth to save your souls. It will be dealt with in every one of your lives. Better now, than later," says the Lord!

Chapter 6 - South Gate

Having been ousted out of the north, east and west gates by the rebuking of the Spirit of the Lord, I found myself at the south gate of the temple in my God-given vision of his Son, Jesus Christ, on the cross. Through the sorrow and the anguish I was enduring in this vision of our Lord and Savior, Jesus Christ, I did everything I could in my effort to hold back tears as I intently looked at my Savior's nail-pierced feet. It felt as though I could hardly breathe anymore.

I was on the verge of passing out again like I did when the vision first started. I didn't even get the chance to be overcome with guilt and sorrow over seeing my Savior's pierced, crowned head, and nail-pierced hands as I experienced the sorrow overcoming my soul, kneeling on both knees at the foot of the cross. I was humbled to the lowest part of the cross my Lord and Savior was left to die on for me, and for the sins of the world.

As I looked up at the sacrificed Lamb, I saw the body of the Good Shepherd laying down His life for His sheep. I saw the whole being of my God manifested in the form of man, the Savior of mankind. It was then that I recalled what Jesus Christ did before he was to endure his suffering for the sins of the world. Jesus knew that the Father had put all things under his power, and that he had come from God, and was returning to God.

He got up from the meal, took off his outer clothing, and wrapped a towel around his waist. After that, he poured water into a basin and began to wash His disciples' feet, drying them with the towel that was wrapped around Him.

He came to Simon Peter, who said to Him,

"Lord, are you going to wash my feet?"

Jesus replied, "You do not realize now what I am doing, but later you will understand."

"No," said Peter, "You shall never wash my feet." Jesus answered, "Unless I wash you, you have no part with me."

"Then, Lord," Simon Peter replied, "not just my feet but my hands and my head as well!"

"Jesus answered, "Those who have had a bath need only to wash their feet; their whole body is clean. And you are clean, though not every one of you." For he knew who was going to betray Him, and that is why he said not everyone was clean."   *(John 13:3-11 NIV)*

"You get that? Not everyone was clean! He had a betrayer with Him all along his journey on this earth like he does even now in this day and age among ALL his so-called followers."

"So, if my Son had a betrayer in his life, where in your right mind are you so overcome with betrayal in your life? You get betrayed out of unfaithfulness and you become a zombie? Actually if you had me first in your life as I should be," says the Lord, "betrayal wouldn't even be an issue in your life. I would NEVER betray you," says the Lord!

"If you can see yourself at the foot of cross, with Jesus Christ hanging there, do you know what would be happening to you? The blood my Son shed on the cross went in only one direction - downward. Being humble before me, the Lord your God, at the foot of the cross would allow my Son, Jesus Christ's, blood to fall on you in your time of prayer and repentance. If you were sincere in your repentance towards me, the Lord your God, while you pray in a remorseful state, your cry would be honored by your Father in heaven."

"Why? Because as you literally cry unto me, maybe a drop of my Son's blood would fall into your mouth while you sincerely pray and totally set you free from the bondage of sin, heartache and sorrow in your life. I specifically told all of you:

"I declare to you brothers and sisters, that flesh and blood cannot inherit the kingdom of God, nor does the perishable inherit the imperishable."

(1 Corinthians 15:50 NIV)

"But sincerely humbled at the foot of the cross at my Son's feet would allow my Son's words to truly come alive in you. His blood is from his own flesh that he gave as your sacrifice unto the salvation of your souls."

"So Jesus said again, I tell you the truth, unless you eat the flesh of the Son of man and drink his blood, you cannot have eternal life within you. But anyone who eats my flesh and drinks my blood has eternal life, and I will raise that person up at the last day. For my flesh is true food, and my blood is true drink. Anyone who eats my flesh and drinks my blood remains in me, and I in Him. I live because of the Living Father who sent me in the same way, anyone who feeds on me will live because of me."   *(John 6:53-57 NLT)*

"Maybe you should get off your religious ceremonial sacrifices and truly sacrifice your total being to me," says the Lord! "You eat an imaginary piece of bread, and drink an imaginary wine in your religious sacrifices at your man made an altars of church by faith, yet you totally refuse to give yourselves to me whole heartedly, where you can eat the flesh of the Son of Man, and drink his blood, and have eternal life."

"That is why when you leave your church services, nothing ever changes in your suppressed lives. You get inspired and energized, and motivated from a spoken word you heard which is good in its own way. Or you heard the same old message of live right for God and all else falls into place. But you still have those tormenting spirits living in your heart, souls and minds that keep you in fear, shame, regret, and uncertain about your own personal life. Especially if what you did was right, and you still get betrayed and let down, or taken advantage of."

"I challenge you to come to the foot of the cross where my Son, Jesus Christ, hung for you and your salvation of your souls. There is power in the blood of my Son Jesus Christ, that no church, religion, belief, or faith can give you in this world to overcome all the power of the enemy (Satan) in your life. And trust Me, you are going to need it in the coming days!"

"It's going to be a power you are going to need that surpasses any power you have ever seen in the evidence of miracles, signs and wonders performed by me, the Holy Spirit! It will be a power that you will have to have to resist the presence of the evil one who will be in this world, but for only ONE purpose! Not the presence of evil that is now in the world that causes people to sin, and commit sin. It will be an evil that will literally take you out of existence! In other words kill you! Literally! For believing in me, and serving me with your life, and your faith."

"It will be a time of persecution you wouldn't have ever imagined. A time of persecution, not because you commit sin and live in sin. The church already persecutes my people in that area. It will be a time of persecution because you wholeheartedly love me, and worship me with your whole heart."

"Oh I go through that already, Lord!"

"Really? Is it because you love me, or the way you handle yourself in living your life while saying you follow me? No! This persecution that is going to take place will be a very bold act of faith one is going to have to stand on! Like you do for your children you love! That's even if you know who your children are! Like you do your addictions of drugs and alcohol you love so much, that you come up with every excuse you can to defend your addiction. Like the way you defend your abuser saying you love them to others who tell you to leave them."

"I think it's time to step up your faith in me, the Lord your God, as you were told at the very beginning of this message. Sharpen your faith and love in me," says the Lord! "You are going to need it! Trust me, I am not trying to put fear in you over what's coming in the future. Actually, I am trying to get you to get up off your complacent mentalities over what is going on in your world right before your very eyes. You are acting like people who do nothing but sleep while the sun is shining very brightly outside. I can see why one sleeps if they work overnight. But the irony to this sleep thing is the majority of the human race sleeps at night. Very common! But does that mean you have to sleep while night rules the day in this life you live?"

"What?"

"I am talking about the life you live for me! Must you sleep while night rules the world you live in? Don't you remember my Son saying something of that sort? I guess not!

"Jesus answered, 'Are there not twelve hours of daylight? Anyone who walks in the daytime will not stumble, for he sees by this world's light. It is when a person walks at night that they stumble, for the have no light.'" (John 11:9-10 NIV)

It goes on to say,

"I am the light of the world!" (John 8:12)

"Whether it's daytime, or nighttime in this life you live. In fact, if you remember when my servant prophet was given the vision of the temple of the Lord his God and the Lamb, it wasn't mentioned about the city (heaven) they were in. It reads,

91

"The city does not need the sun or the moon to shine on it, for the glory of God gives it light, and the Lamb is its lamp."   *(Revelation 21:23 NIV)*

"I need to ask you something! If it's dark in the room you are in and you want to look at something, or see something what do you do in order to get a clear vision of what you are wanting to see? You light a lamp or a light, right? Well, since I am the light of the world, yet your world seems like it's full of darkness, my Son, Jesus Christ, is the very lamp you need in this dark world you live in! Why? It is written,

"And they overcame and conquered Him because of the blood of the Lamb and because of the word of their testimony, for they did not love their life and renounce their faith even when faced with death."   *(Revelation 12:11 AMP)*

But guess what? There are not very many of you who even think of coming to the foot of the cross for the simple reason being you're lazy and complacent with your religious kingdom empires you have built in your own names of religions, faiths and denominations. Not to mention Christianity! The kingdom that has convinced itself, and come to the conclusion that no such persecution, or judgments will come upon the face of this earth until they (true believers) are removed out of the way for those deserving punishment for not living the way they should've been living for God in heaven."

"Seriously! Listen to yourselves! How can people not living for me, be persecuted because of me? They have nothing to do with me! Satan's got them where he wants them. The devil doesn't want his own followers. He's after those who are not his followers! Use your common sense, if you have any! I told my apostle Peter, "…a person who has had a bath, needs only to wash his feet, his whole body is clean, though not everyone of you." Now mind you, a clean body that just got out of the tub is clean. But the minute they step out of the tub, your feet get dirty; even if you step onto a towel, or mat on the floor; even if you put house shoes on to walk around in, eventually your feet touch the floor surface and get dirty after you just had a bath. Even if you put your feet into your house shoes you wore already, they have dust on them you can't even see, dirt your feet come in contact with."

"Sort of like my people who go to church, but have no change of heart. They look clean in the church wardrobe coming out of their man-made temples, yet inwardly they are just as evil in my eyes as they were before they even went to church. That is what millions of you do in your faith walk with me. You accept my mercy, love and forgiveness that cleanses your soul and being; yet, you walk into anything, and everything you shouldn't be walking into."

"That is why you need to wash your feet when you enter into my temple. You don't like people tracking mud and dirt all into your place of living, do you? That's what you do with your arrogant attitudes towards your salvation in me: 'Come as you are, the Lord loves you!'"

"Yes, I do! That doesn't mean you are going to see me in the after-life."

"What?"

"Now, brothers, I know that you acted in ignorance, as did your leaders. But this is how God fulfilled what he had foretold through all the prophets, saying that his Christ would suffer. Repent then and turn to God, so that your sins may be wiped out, that the times of refreshing may come from the Lord, and that he may send the Christ, who he has appointed to you — even Jesus. He must remain in heaven until the time comes for God to restore everything, as he promised long ago through his holy prophets. For Moses said, The Lord your God will raise up for you a prophet like me from among your own people you must listen to everything he tells you. Anyone who does not listen to Him will be completely cut off from among his people." *(Acts 3:17-23 NIV)*

"Let me start with the last portion of this passage of scripture I just shared with you. The passage that says, *"Anyone who does not listen to Him will completely be cut off from his people."* *(Acts 3:23 NIV)*

93

That goes for everyone in general! Followers, and non-followers alike! Believers, and non-believers! Church going, or not! Righteous, and unrighteous! No favoritism," says the Lord!

"For God does not show favoritism   *(Romans 2:11 NIV)*

"You see that word 'ANYONE'? It's meant for anyone who has a will to find me in order for me to help them in their life. I only said that for you condemning Christians who are wanting nothing more than my impending judgments on this world for its deeds of sins. Well, judging my people falls into that category too! You came to the cross to receive your forgiveness, and I cleansed you by washing you. Even your feet! But what did you do after leaving the cross? You went and dirtied your feet by walking in the valley of condemnation unto my people! You condemn everyone to hell for everything that is in their lives that shouldn't be. Then you come to me in your own ways of faith without coming to the foot of the cross to repent of your evil hearted hearts that you very well know I saved you through grace and mercy! Yet you can't give it to others like I gave it to you."

"You are just wanting my return to take place, just to get the hell away from those who live totally opposite of what you live. And you who come to me through the east and west gates of my temple without ever changing your evil-spirit, perverted hearts of perversion and religions. What shall I do with you? That is why I said: ANYONE who does not listen to me will be completely cut off from among my people. That is why I started with this portion of my message to you by saying to you,

"Now, brothers, I know that you acted in ignorance as did your leaders."

(Acts 3:17 NIV)

"You can't help it you were brought up through religion as a child of mine. You respectively went where your parents took you, even if you didn't want to go. The majority of you knew while growing up in church there had to be more than what met the eye as far as surviving in this wicked, degraded world you live in. That goes for the way you were brought up in your homes too! That's if you even had a place you called home, in this perverted divided generation."

"So like everyone else in this life you live, you set out on an adventure to find that peace and contentment everyone desires to have within themselves and their being. So you went here and there, and everywhere looking for that happiness and peace in this world you needed. You search every venue within your own interest except in ME," says the Lord! "You even went to where you had no business going! Now your life is in shambles, and in ruins and totally full of darkness and confusion, thus leaving you in tears of sorrow and anguish, right along with broken-heartedness. Sort of like this world was what it first began. You ever read how the world was in the beginning? Probably not! It was in the shape that most of your lives are in."

"In the beginning, God created the heavens and the earth. Now the earth was formless and empty, darkness was over the surface of the deep, and the Spirit of God was hovering over the waters."   *(Genesis 1:1-2 NIV)*

"Your life by now has no solid shape to it whatsoever, leaving it formless and empty. You have this void of emptiness within your soul and spirit being. So now darkness covers the face of the deep. In other words, your inner being has no vision of what may lie ahead for you. You are totally blind in what to do, or which way to go! Total insecurity in your life even though all you are wanting is happiness and peace in your life."

"So where is God in all my darkness and confusion of uncertainty? Like the scripture says, the Spirit of God was hovering over the waters! In other words amidst all your tears of broken-heartedness, loneliness, isolation, and uncertainty, I am there for you yet you won't let me in your heart and life because of your fears of me resenting you like people have resented you all your life."

"That goes for you too, my so-called church! You cry unto me over all the wickedness this world is portraying before you while you anxiously await my return in order to get the hell out of dodge and watch me pour out my wrath on everyone else. Yet this whole time, my Spirit hovers over the waters -- the cries of my people, the body of Christ -- instead of you letting me in to be used of you."

"But this is how God fulfilled what he foretold through all the prophets, saying that his Christ would suffer."   *(Acts 3:18 NIV)*

"You read that passage of Christ's suffering, and you go to the cross he endured for mankind. What if I told you he endured that cross more for you, my followers that he did mankind in general. Yes, he died for the sins of the world as the scriptures testify. But you should pay more attention to who my Son is, instead of who he was! Why? Because,

"Jesus Christ is the same yesterday, today and forever."   *(Hebrews 13:8 NIV)*

"He told you Himself in his word,

"I am not referring to all of you; I know those I have chosen. But this is to fulfill the scripture: He who shares my bread has lifted up his heel against me."
                                       (John 13:18 NIV)

"In other words, you have partaken in everything that pertains itself to me in this world you live in: Church, righteous living, faith and knowledge of me, religious rituals and customs, traditions, etc, etc. You even claim to be my follower! Yet you hate your brothers and sisters of society for whatever reason you carry within you, thus wishing judgments on them of me," says the Lord.

"While I was with them, I protected them and kept them safe by the name you gave me. None has been lost except the one doomed to destruction so that scripture would be fulfilled."   *(John 17:12 NIV)*

"So, if anyone is lost and doomed to destruction, it will happen only to fulfill scripture that says it must happen this way. So, if one chooses not to live for me, scripture will be fulfilled of them being doomed to destruction. Likewise, if one chooses to live for me, yet lives totally opposite of what they were taught to do in me, the scripture will be fulfilled in their doom to destruction."

"You remember those coming into the kingdom through the east and west gates? They would be millions! But the subjects will be thrown out of the kingdom. That was the meaning of the saying everyone who does not listen to Him, my Son, will be completely cut off."

"That leads me to tell you why Jesus Christ must remain in heaven until the time comes for God to restore everything. If God doesn't restore everything, you wouldn't want Jesus Christ to come yet, would you?"

"I see no possible restoration in this world Lord, according to biblical prophecy."

"That is why I am having this message delivered to you. This isn't about the world you are living in, in general. This is about YOU! What if you are not even here when I come for my people again? Do you think you will get into my kingdom when I come for you, if all you had your mind set on was me sending judgments into the world against all the evil and wickedness amidst you?"

"What would it matter to you if you are called into my presence while the world is still going? What should I do with you then, for being in that mode of expectant judgment against the evil in this world, instead of you being in expectancy of my coming to you? Do you understand what I am pointing out to you? It's your hearts I am looking at," says the Lord!

"Repent, then, and turn to God, so that your sins may be wiped out, that the times of refreshing may come from the Lord, and that he may send the Christ,

who has been appointed FOR YOU!"   *(Acts 3:19-20 NIV)*

"That is why he must remain in heaven until the time comes for me to restore everything. He must remain in heaven until the time comes for God to restore everything, as he promised long ago through his holy prophets." (Acts 3:21 NIV)

"So, as you picture my Son Jesus Christ sitting in heaven on his glorious throne let me enlighten you on where my Son Jesus Christ really should be. He is totally omnipresent! This means He is everywhere in the power of the Spirit! Everywhere he can be, except inside of you, my people!"

"What?"

"Yes, except you! Look,

"Once, having been asked by the Pharisees when the kingdom of God would come, Jesus replied, 'The kingdom of God does not come with careful observation, nor will people say, Here it is, or There it is, because the kingdom of God IS WITHIN YOU.'"   *(Luke 17:20-21 NIV)*

"The religious people of then, like the religious people of now, have to see things spoken of before they believe in them. So they asked my Son when the kingdom of God was coming. He told them, the kingdom of God wasn't going to come where one could observe it with careful observation. Nor were people going to say, here it is! Or, there it is!"

"But guess what? People do say that! 'Come to this church, and you will find God! Go to that church, and you will find God! Believe in this religion, or that religion, or this faith, and that faith, and you will find God!'"

"Liars! The kingdom of God is within you. So, who rules your life? Who is king over your life, which is my kingdom within you that I am putting together for eternity? So now I have made it clear to you that my kingdom is within you, right? I hope so! Because that is where

Jesus Christ, my Son, belongs, and should remain until the time comes for God to restore everything."

"So if nothing has been restored in your life, or even in your churches for that matter, it must be that my Son isn't where he belongs. He must remain IN YOU in order for everything to be restored. If you want me to come for you my people in your so-called rapture, then let my Son Jesus Christ rule your life in doing so. It will be then that you will know that the ONLY coming that will take place of my Son will be A SECOND COMING!"

"Then you will see through my Son's tear-filled eyes why I haven't come yet for my people! You would understand what was written about my Son through the prophet Jeremiah. He said,

"Since my people are crushed, I am crushed; I mourn, and horror grips me."
(Jeremiah 8:21 NIV)

"Or as my prophet Ezekiel testified in my written word,

"Do you think that I like to see wicked people die?" says the Sovereign Lord. "Of course not! I want them to turn from their wicked ways and live."
(Ezekiel 18:23 NLT)

"That goes for you followers of mine, too, who psychologically convince yourselves going to church is your ticket to heaven, while you totally disgrace my Son's sacrifice on the cross for your soul's eternal life. It cost Him EVERYTHING! His life included!"

"In the past, God overlooked such ignorance, but now he commands all people everywhere to repent. For he has set a day when he will judge the world with justice by the man he has appointed. He has given proof of this to all men by raising Him from the dead.   *(Acts 17:30-31 NIV)*

"Of course, you know the man I appointed to judge the world, don't you? Tell me you don't! It is my Son, Jesus Christ! He already judged every one of you, finding all of you not guilty of doing anything wrong in his eyes of Love, grace, and mercy through his death on the cross. But what have you done with his Love, mercy, and grace? You take it as a free pass to heaven to come into my kingdom as you are!"

"So be it! You will find out differently when you get here. Why? Because you have not humbled yourself before me like my Son did for you and your messed up life in my presence. He was obedient unto the death of the cross! He point blank told all of you,

"… and anyone who does not take up his cross and follow me is not worthy of me." (Matthew 10:38, 16:24) (Mark 8:34) (Luke 9:23, 14:27 NIV)

"So if you're thinking going to church as much as you do and living a life of righteousness towards me the Lord your God can get you into heaven you need an attitude adjustment. My Son also said to all of you,

"Whoever acknowledges me before men, I will also acknowledge Him before my Father in heaven. But whoever disowns me before men, I will disown Him before my Father in heaven." (Matthew 10:32-33; Luke 12:8-9 NIV)

"We do acknowledge you, Lord! That's why we go to church and live our lives as best as we can, according to your word!"

"Then why do you condemn everyone elsewhere who isn't like you in your so-called faith in me as your Lord and Savior? That's how you acknowledge me in your life? A God who sends people to hell, when in reality, I died for the sins of the world."

"That is why we are at the south gate of the temple. This is the gate where my Son's pierced feet are. The foot of the cross is the narrowest gate of all the gate entrances to my temple. One foot nailed directly on top of the other is a narrower margin in comparison to the width of one's head as far as the body goes."

"The head is the source where knowledge enters into one's mind.

This is why all of you know of me, and about me by what you have heard of me taught to you. The east and west gates are my love, grace, mercy, and forgiveness given unto mankind. But to know me personally comes only to those who humble themselves at the foot of the cross where they show me a willingness to humble themselves before me where they can be exalted of me, in truly knowing me."

"That is why my Son pleaded with all of you,

"Enter through the narrow gate. For wide is the gate and broad is the road that leads to destruction, and many enter through it. But small is the gate and narrow the road that leads to life, and only a few find it." (Matthew 7:13-14 NIV)

"Why?"

"Therefore Jesus said again, I tell you the truth, I AM the gate for the sheep. All whoever came before me were thieves and robbers, but the sheep did not listen to them. I am the gate; whoever enters through me will be saved. He will come in and go out and find pasture." (John 10:7-9 NIV)

That is why you should take my word to heart when you read into it! Many of you hold onto my promised word that says,

"The Lord is my Shepherd, I lack nothing." (Psalm 23:1 NIV)

"Yet you seem to be lacking everything in your life. Not materialistically, but within your souls. As far as material needs,

"The poor you will always have with you, but you will not always have me."
(Matthew 26:11 NIV)

"Of course, many of you take that literally and accept it that you will never advance in prosperity. That's not what it means! I wish you would take the rest of my written word that seriously. The poverty I speak of is the soul of my people! Why? You realize all who ever came, or come before me are thieves and robbers, and my sheep do not listen to those voices. Religions were here way before I came.

Sacrificial offerings were here before I ever showed up. Selfish, self-centered, evil non-repentant hearts were here before I came. Everything in this world you look to for Hope was here before I showed up! So what choice does that leave you in finding a way to heaven? You forgot, didn't you? I told you,

"Jesus answered, I am the way and the truth and the life. NO ONE comes to the Father except through me." (John 14:6 NIV)

"That is why I am wanting you to come to the foot of the cross where you will literally humble yourself before me, where I can exalt you. Listen,

"When someone invites you to a wedding feast, do not take the place of honor, for a person more distinguished than you may have been invited. If so, the host who invited both of you will come and say to you, Give this man your seat! Then, humiliated, you will have to take the least important place." (Luke 14:8-9 NIV)

"Remember how you get ready for the futuristic wedding? Now you will see how I will expect you to attend the wedding. Every one of you are invited to my Son's wedding feast! That's everybody in this world. The day of the Marriage Supper of the Lamb, I mentioned earlier in my message to you."

"Then the angel said to me, Write: Blessed are those who are invited to the wedding supper of the Lamb! And he added, These are the true words of God." (Revelation 19:9 NIV)

"So, you religious bigots, and arrogant righteous believers need to think twice before you try and take all the front row seats in my kingdom with your arrogant attitudes of condemnation on everyone else in this dying world you live in."

"But when you are invited, take the lowest place, so that when your host comes, he

will say to you, Friend, move up to a better place. Then you will be honored in the presence of all your fellow guests. For everyone who exalts Himself will be humbled, and he who humbles Himself will be exalted." (Luke 14:10-11 NIV)

"Therefore I say to you all of you, my beloved people : if my people, who are called by my name, will humble themselves and pray and seek my face and turn from their wicked ways, then I, will hear from heaven and will forgive their sin and will heal their land."   *(2 Chronicles 7:14 NIV)*

"I am personally calling every one of you my children to come unto me where I can give you rest unto your burdened and hurting souls. It has nothing to do with a perfection lifestyle of living. It's more of me watching you accept my Son, Jesus Christ's, sacrifice for you on the cross, than for you to walk away thinking you can find your own way into my kingdom!"

"That is why it is written: Therefore, I urge you, brothers and sisters, in view of God's mercy, to offer your bodies as a living sacrifice, holy and pleasing to God – this is your TRUE and PROPER worship. Do not confirm to the pattern of this world, but be transformed by the renewing of your mind. Then you will be able to test and approve what God's will is – his good, pleasing and perfect will. For by the grace given me I say to every one of you: DO NOT THINK of yourself more highly than you ought, but think of yourself with sober judgment, in accordance with the faith God has distributed to each of you."

(Romans 12:1-3 NIV)

"That goes for everybody, Church going, or not! Renew your attitude in the way you live your lives in my presence," says the Lord! "This is about my Son who hung on the cross for every one of you. So, come to the foot of the cross the South gate of the temple where my Son, Jesus Christ, hung as your sacrifice."

"Now my eyes will be open and my ears attentive to the prayers offered in this place. I have chosen this temple so that my name may be there forever. My eyes and my heart will always be there."   *(2 Chronicles 7:15-16 NIV)*

"That at the Name of JESUS EVERY KNEE should bow, in heaven and on earth and under the earth, and EVERY TONGUE CONFESS that Jesus Christ is Lord, to the glory of God the Father."

(Philippians 2:10-11 NIV)

Chapter 7 - The Kings of the Medes

"Now! You have been given insight to the narrow gate (the South gate) that leads to life, and few there are who find it! Why? Selfishness my child! Total Selfishness! Even by my so called followers, who can't find the strength to come to the foot of the cross in order to enter into my kingdom for the sake of THEIR religions, and self-wills."

"Of course, when I say enter my kingdom you instinctively look to the future: the future of one passing away in this life. They die! You die! But let me say to you: the future is NOW! This means this very day if I demand your life from you where will you end up? With me in my kingdom? Or in outer darkness where there will be weeping and gnashing of teeth?"

"Religion **WILL NOT** save you from hell and eternal darkness. Church will not save you! Righteous living will not save you! And, sure as hell itself, self-will has never saved anyone! Is this a threat? NO! It's a fact of what is about to take place in this very world you live in. Stop playing ritual games with me," says the Lord! "I told you in the beginning of this message:

"Sharpen the arrows, take up the shields! The Lord has stirred up the kings of the Medes, because his purpose is to destroy Babylon. The Lord will take vengeance for his temple." *(Jeremiah 51:11 NIV)*

"I shared with you who the kings of the Medes were earlier in this message. They are the ancestors of the modern day Turks in your world you live in today. From that very same region, with the very same purpose, is their mission of then, to now. If you were familiar with my word you would see Media and Persia are going to play out a BIG part of end time prophesies. They symbolize the image of a ram my prophet Daniel had a vision of that pertains to the end of time."

"In the third year of King Belshazzar's reign, I, Daniel, had a vision, after the one that had already appeared to me. In my vision I saw myself in the citadel of Susa in the province of Elam in the vision I was beside the Ulai Canal. I looked up, and there before me was a ram with two horns, standing beside the canal, and the horns were long. One of the horns was longer than the other but grew up later. I watched the ram as he charged towards the west and the north and the south. No animal could stand against Him, and none could rescue from his power. <u>HE DID AS HE PLEASED</u> and became great."   (Daniel 8:1-4 NIV)

In the time of the end which you are in now as I speak there will be world rulers that will come into power that have no intentions of good but only evil! That evil is nothing more than wanting to be a world leader who want to rule your lives in this world. Shouldn't surprise you considering some of the leaders you have had in recent years, even in your own nation you call, the United States of America: Presidents, congressmen, state representatives, Supreme Court justices, etc. Only if you were united as your name says you are America, wouldn't have all the problems it does," says the Lord! "Why did I say that? Because I will allow world leaders to do as they please according to their own evil desires according to my plans and purposes in this world you live in, just to fulfill end time prophecies spoken of by my TRUE prophets in the Old Testament."

"Even very recent past presidents in your own nation, the United States of America, that would rather worship another god, other than the only **TRUE GOD**, my Son, Jesus Christ, the image of the invisible God. (Colossians 1:15)"

"This doesn't sound like something God would allow! Allowing it to happen if it's going to affect and hurt his people."

"Why not? I allow you to do as you please in your own personal lives regardless how many people you hurt in the process, and do you care? HELL NO! Do I wipe you off of the face of the earth for being such a cowardly, possessed, evil spirit? No, I don't! Why? Because in most cases of evil hearted people ruining the lives of innocent people, my purpose is fulfilled in other people's lives through your selfish evil heartedness."

"Those you hurt and ruin their lives in your evil quest are broken and wounded by your evil behavior in their lives, and in their times of darkness and sorrow, they cry out to me for salvation. And guess what? I saved them! And that becomes their testimony. I, the Lord your God, used you being an evil coward possessed by a spirit of hell as a stepping stone unto my glory in my child's life you ruined and destroyed."

"That includes you leaders in the church pulpits who have ruined millions of *my people* with your deceptive messages of a quote rapture theory! My Prophet Daniel saw many different kinds of animals and beasts that will appear on the earth you live in. This ram he saw will be a kingdom that will power itself throughout the world through evil acts of crime, terrorism, and self-will!"

"Deceptive witchcraft, more potent than any of you could have ever imagined is something you are getting acquainted with already in this world you live in. And I, the Lord your God, will allow it? If you say so! Yes, I said so! I just stir up evil spirits to get things done prophetically that otherwise wouldn't get done. I, myself, the Lord your God, through the power of the Holy Spirit, have been trying to stir myself up in each and every one of you, *my people,* who claim to know me as the Lord and Savior of your life, to get this world where it's supposed to be."

"But what are you doing? You are literally quenching my Holy Spirit, condemning everybody to hell for their sins. And the rest of you are quenching my Holy Spirit by hardening your hearts towards me with unrepentant hearts while confessing me as your Lord and Savior, Jesus Christ! And then I have my beautiful church who sits in the spirit of complacency, awaiting my return! You have become my lukewarm church that I am about to spit out of my mouth," says the Spirit of the Lord!

"So, what choice do I have in the matter? The choice I have made this very day. I will stir up the spirit of the kings of the Medes! They will come to life stronger than they have in recent years through terrorist attacks against all of you!"

"This doesn't sound like God talking!"

"Really! Why not? I told you what the purpose of my stirring up the spirit of the Medes was. To destroy Babylon - your kingdoms of religions, faiths and denominations! Your kingdoms of Babylonian self-willed lives that crave the things of this world thus making you a worshippers of gold, wood, stone, and silver just to name a few. If you would hear what I am trying to tell you, you would see my love, mercy and grace for you in this message."

"My Son told you what was going to be going on in this world, before his return. For once let's leave sin out of the picture in what he told you of before his return. Sin in this world is forever going to stay in its place. It's like a fog over the earth that you just have to see your way through without it affecting you, or taking you hostage. It's only allowed to live in you, IF YOU allow it to live in you."

"I told you already when my Son Jesus Christ said it is finished while on the cross he meant the atonement of sin was taken care of. So anyone who wants to be forgiven, was/is forgiven through his sacrifice. But since what he did wasn't good enough for the majority of you we are talking about the spirit of Babylon here!"

"For the Son of Man in his <u>DAY</u> will be like the Lightning that flashes and lights up the sky from one end to the other. But first <u>he must suffer many things and be rejected by this generation.</u> Just as it was in the days of Noah, so also will it be in the days of the Son of Man. People were eating, drinking, marrying and being given in marriage up to the day Noah entered the ark. Then the flood destroyed them all. It was the same in the days of Lot. People were eating and drinking, buying and selling, planting and building. But the day Lot left Sodom, fire and sulphur rained down from heaven and destroyed them all. It will be just like that the day the Son of Man is revealed."   *(Luke 17:24-30 NIV)*

"Apart from what was going on in the lives of *my people* then, with regard to what you consider sin, the main aspect that had to be dealt with was **SELF-LIVING.** In other words, nobody was living for me, the Lord God of all creation! Do you think all the people were indulged in what everybody else was doing as far as sins were concerned in Noah's time, or Lot's time? It wasn't about what the people were doing as far as their own personal lives of pleasure and lust cravings of the body. Especially in Lot's day! It was more of the notion that mankind had become so consumed with itself, (lovers of themselves), to the point it had literally put me, the Lord their God, on the back burner."

"Seriously! Look at it now in this day and age you are living in! Are all of you perverts? Are all of you pedophiles, murderers, or thieves? Of course not! Do all of you condemn everybody to hell over their lifestyles? No, not really, just church going people do that! If you go to church, why do you do that? Even those you consider sinners in your own eyes love sinners!"

"If you love those who love you, what credit is that to you? Even sinners love those who love them."   *(Luke 6:32 NIV)*

"Are all of you self-seekers in this life you live? Lovers of yourselves, more than lovers of your God in heaven who created you, died for you, to free you from your selfish spirit of living for yourself? Yes, most certainly! All of you are self-seekers, in one way or another, fashion, or form. Even you followers of mine do that!"

"So! In your self-seeking efforts am I, the Lord your God of heaven, included in your efforts of your self-centered lifestyles? Hell no! I just told you that you have me on the back burner! Your first priorities are, 'I want a new house! I want more money! I want a new car! I want a new wife, or husband! I want to be rich! I just want to party and have fun! I want to be the best minister/ preacher where everybody comes to me to hear me teach the word of the Lord, because no one teaches like I do!'"

"Guess what? For having me on the back burner in your lives I am about to light the front burners of your lives to show you where I should be in your lives, instead of where you have me," says the Lord! "Then you will know what is written about Babylon's future and its kingdom that exist in this world."

"Then I heard another voice from heaven say: Come out of her, my people, so that you will not share in her sins, so that you will not receive any of her plagues for her sins are piled up to heaven, and God has remembered her crimes."
(Revelation 18:4-5 NIV)

"That is why I told you at the beginning of my message to sharpen your arrows, and take up your shields. The armor of God! The TRUE warrior Armor of God! That was why I have showed you the ONLY gate of the temple you are supposed to come in through is the south gate! Where you humble yourself to where I can exalt you! The foot of the cross where the blood of my Son, Jesus Christ flows down to where you are covered by the blood and water of Jesus Christ in these last days on earth. Then, if you are the victim of a terrorist attack you overcome the whole case scenario of their wickedness in trying to rule the world, and people's lives with their wicked acts of violence. They will not overcome you in any way or form whatsoever because you are covered by the blood of the Lamb, Jesus Christ! I told you in my word,

"Do not be afraid of those who can kill the body but cannot kill the soul. Rather, be afraid of the ONE who can destroy both soul and body in hell."

(Matthew 10:28 NIV)

"But what good would that promise in my word do you if you are not covered by the blood of my Son, since you want to come in by some other way other than the way I have provided for you," says, the Lord! "I just told you at the south gate of the temple you have overcome by the blood of the Lamb, and through the word of your testimony."

"People always give testimonies through their words by saying, 'I got Jesus Christ in my heart, and in my life.' They even testify about how I delivered them from addictions, oppression, and depression - all spirits. They're like the people in Moses' day. I did super miraculous signs and wonders and what did they do? They turned to other gods and worshiped them."

"So it is with you, *my people*! You testify with your mouth, yet your heart testifies otherwise. Why? Because you have not come to the foot of the cross where my Son died for you. It not only covers you, and protects you, it also purifies you to stay at the foot of the cross according to your faith. In case you forgot, my Son's side was pierced with a spear, bringing a sudden flow of water and blood that pours itself out of his sacrificed body, thus providing you with pure sanctification and salvation from hell."

"That is why millions of questions loom over many of my promised words. 'If you heal, then why did my loved one die? If you hate evil, why do you allow evil to victimize innocent people? If you are God, where are you?'"

"Surely not in you, my child, as I should be! That is why many haven't overcome anything in their lives by the word of their testimony of claiming to know me; yet are angered in their hearts towards me over something that happened to them in their life. This is because there is no water and blood of the Lamb on them and their life. There is only his love and mercy through the forgiveness of their sins, until they encounter opposition in their life that questions my existence."

"Millions of dedicated, love-filled Americans have shed their blood for this nation, the United States of America, enabling their citizens to have freedom. Would you say their blood is on you and your life? That it makes you live a life of appreciation and dedication to their sacrifice as a true American who fought for their country? Hell no! You just take your freedom for granted in this country and live your lives like devils from hell?"

"Especially you who come into the United States of America from other nations, pushing your faiths and beliefs on everybody else through protest and demonstrations of discrimination against you and your ways. You talk about how everybody hurts your feelings by not accepting your gods, faiths and religions."

"The Truth is, you don't salute the American flag because of their faith in me -- the True God, King of kings, and Lord of lords! If it bothers you that badly that this nation, the United States of America, worships the ONLY TRUE God in Jesus Christ, go back to where you came from."

"What? Come on! This isn't God talking like that! Telling people to go back to their country if they don't want to respect AMERICA's true faith in Him, the Lord God of heaven and earth!"

"Why not? I will say that to all of you who are bothered by *my people* who truly love me, and worship me because I am that I am," says the Lord! "Go back to where you came from! *'From dust you are, to dust you return,'* (Genesis 3:19). Have you ever read that? I told Adam that after he disobeyed me. So, don't be so heart-broken, thinking you are being persecuted over your faiths and religions."

"I would never persecute you," says the Lord! "I will just spew you out of my mouth and tell you, '*Away from me, you evil doer! I never knew you,*'" (Matthew 7:23)!

"What? Why?"

"Because the majority of you don't accept my Son whole-heartedly as you should - just your religions. That's exactly how my Son, Jesus Christ, gets treated by all of you in your society. You accept a religious name and a faith name before you even think of accepting the **ONLY** name I gave mankind unto salvation. I already told you that at the name of my Son, Jesus Christ, <u>EVERY</u> knee will bow, and every tongue confess that my Son, Jesus Christ, is Lord!"

"You must declare that now, from this day forward as you come to the foot of the cross to sharpen your arrows and take up your shields as you will see me take vengeance for my temple," says the Lord! "Why? Because in the vision my prophet Daniel saw was the two horned ram that was pushing west, north and south."

"What about the east, Lord?"

"It cannot go east when it sits in the Middle East! After that, Daniel sees another kingdom come forth in the form of a goat. Daniel had an angelic visitation. The Angel spoke to Daniel, my prophet!"

"*He said: I am going to tell you what will happen later in the time of wrath, because the vision concerns the appointed time of the end. The two horned ram that you saw represents the kings of Media and Persia.*" (Daniel 8:19-20 NIV)

"This is the spirit I am stirring up that will be the beginning of the time of the end. Kingdoms will come and go as you read about them in the book of Daniel in his visions. I want you to know that every terrorist attack that will take place, or takes place, will not always be bombs and explosions going off before your very eyes, or planes crashing into buildings taking out many innocent lives, like you are accustomed to seeing."

"It won't always be vicious, murderous attacks on innocent people either. In case you people of this United States of America haven't noticed, there is a war amidst your children in the education realm of their lives. Actually, it is going on right underneath your noses in your very own public schools. The spirit of Islam is making its presence known in the studies of religions in your children's classrooms."

"Oh, come on, Lord! We have always studied religions, cultures and their history."

"I know," says the Lord! "That is why all of you would rather worship a religion, instead of worshiping my Son, Jesus Christ. You do that in your church gatherings, too," says the Lord! "Teaching the way of religion, instead of the **ONLY WAY** I gave mankind in obtaining the salvation of their souls: Jesus Christ!"

"Do they teach you the way of salvation in all the religions you are taught about? No! Especially the one you call true Christianity! If you dare taught the salvation of my Son, Jesus Christ, in your public schools, chances are you would be imprisoned for it. Yet you can teach the way of salvation in another faith and religion?"

"Do you not see how the system works in the lives you live? It's put into motion by what gets voted in. And either you go with it, or against it. But in all honesty, it probably isn't even that much of an issue to you anyway, because that is how you do all my people, in your religious gatherings in what you call churches."

"You go by what your dioceses of religious faith votes on to teach. You teach doctrine, rituals, customs and traditions. So what difference does it make? What if I told you, eventually you are going to lose your privilege of the freedom you take for granted in this country."

"What? What kind of God are you? Talking that way to us? We are the land of the free, and home of the brave!"

"Yes, I can say, you are very brave in your arrogance towards me, the Lord your God! And free willed in doing what you want, thinking you will get into heaven with that attitude. Though you say, 'You are a God of victory, justice, and salvation! You are a GOD of freedom!' I know I am," says the Lord!

"So, read my word! It means freedom from within your being! Not your life! Haven't you seen the videos popping up in the world you live in, and worship? Social Media! Your own country of America is being accused of building what you would call underground FEMA Camps, right underneath your noses."

"Are the accusations true, Lord? There could be underground bunkers in case of military attacks on our country?"

"If you would look into my word and see what is prophetically written you could answer your own curiosity. But NOOO! You are going to be raptured out of the way of all the evil coming into the world. So, as you wait upon my return, they build into the future."

"Actually, that is what you should be doing yourselves, as my believers. This world is getting ready to control your country right along with all the other countries under a ONE WORLD government system. Sort of like you have been trying to do with the gospel of MY Lord Jesus Christ! This world leader coming onto the scene in this out of control world is going to establish a world peace like no other man has ever established in the entire existence of mankind. Not even my Son, Jesus Christ, was able to conquer that task."

"Why? Because he didn't come to do that. He came to save and deliver you out of this world! He came to give you peace! But not as the world gives! Read my word and you will see what I am talking about. But you failed to accept me, the Holy Spirit, the Spirit of truth! You choose religions and faiths over me," says the Lord your God!

"Don't you see the spirit of the anti-Christ already marshaling his forces and troops together in his conquest for world supremacy? It is right in your faces! When I told all of you, whenever all these things begin to happen lift up your heads, your redemption draws near. I meant for you to stop slouching around taking your salvation for granted, like you do your freedom in this country you live in you call the United States of America. Fight to take America back if you want! You might obtain your victory, and in doing so, it will be for a very, very short time and a season."

"Well, that sounds very encouraging, Lord! A very, very short time and a season?"

"Yes, a very, very short time and season! You have elections every four years in your country. What do you think Jesus meant when he said, '…brother will betray brother, (Matthew 10:21 NLT),' and a man his own family? Your own government will do this in the time of the end, because of these non-stop liberals. You think these liberals around you are going to sit still and quiet over your victory of a Christian President running this nation?"

"Hell, no! They are not like you are in my churches across this nation: complacent and relaxed, knowing their God in heaven wins in the end! I do win in the end, but not in this world! I will come to defeat every enemy on the face of the earth that is in my face that has totally rejected my Son, Jesus Christ! That includes millions of you who worship your doctrines of religion, **ALL OF YOU**! Then they will be tossed out of my presence into outer darkness where there will be weeping and gnashing of teeth."

"That is what you should concern yourselves with, if you want to get to the bottom of what all is going on around you. I AM is about to take vengeance for his resurrected temple: my Son, Jesus Christ! That is why these liberals pray to their gods non-stop through sacrifices and total devotional worship."

"For crying out loud! You have but ONE GOD to call upon – **ME** - - and you don't even make an effort to call upon me. You can't even make time for prayer in your non-purposed lives. The ruler of this world, Satan, knows that of you. That was why the question was asked:

*"Why do the nations conspire and the people's plot in vain? The kings of the earth rise up and the rulers band together against the Lord and against his anointed, saying, Let us break their chains and throw off their shackles. The One enthroned in heaven laughs; the Lord scoffs at them. He rebukes them in his anger and terrifies them in his wrath, saying, I have installed my king on Zion, my holy mountain. I will proclaim the Lord's decree: He said to me, You are my Son; today I have become **your Father**."* (Psalm 2:1-7 NIV)

"Religions have rules and standards one goes by to get into heaven. My Son, Jesus Christ, wasn't, and isn't, a religion with rules. He said,

"Jesus answered, I am the way, and the truth and the life. No one comes to the Father except through me." (John 14:6 NIV)

"You just give yourself to me, Jesus Christ, **WHOLE HEARTEDLY**! Just teach your children that about me, as you should, and they shouldn't be confused over different religions, and faiths they are taught about, right?"

"Sure, Lord! No problem!"

"Really? First you have to be there for them. Try that first! How can they listen to you if you don't even make time for them to hear you? You are nowhere around, since you are so caught up in yourself."

"Well, I would Lord, but my ex won't let me near my kids!"

"You have laws that give you rights to your kids…use them! Or are you too busy with your new-found lover in your life, who rules your life?"

"Well, I just don't want any trouble, Lord. So I stay away from it."

"Really? Then how did you get yourself into your mess in the first place, if you just wanted to stay away from trouble?"

"That's what all my so-called followers are going to be asking themselves when these days of vengeance for my temple take place. 'How did we get into all this evil mess that is going on, if all we ever did was stay away from it?' All it takes is an effort of will power on your part in using those laws. This is the same will power effort you used in cheating on your spouse, or your lover, in the first place that cause them to build an embankment against you on every side in you not being able to see your children."

"Even when your children are with you, you can't even teach them to respect you through discipline. You spare the rod, and spoil the child. Because they are hurt over their parents fighting with each other. Or you don't want them doing without like you did growing up! Whatever your reason is in not disciplining is not good enough."

"Why? Getting back to school and education! It leaves the teachers in your public schools with their hands tied behind their backs as far as corporal punishment goes. They can't touch your child through discipline, either, or you will sue the school! So disruption takes place in the classrooms. The majority of your youth end up with little education, and more free time to spend in juvenile centers."

"It's all about tax incentives school districts receive from the government over how many children attend class on a regular basis. Money! That's all your children are: tax incentives. That is how the education curriculum is to your teachers in your education realm of life. It's dictated through a government system that says: teach them what we tell you to teach them; otherwise, forfeit your job, and your career. Go find another job!"

"It's your liberals amongst you who push their weight around and take every one of you captive with their ways. So, yes, those who do not honor me in Spirit and in truth way outnumber those that do. Sadly, that's how it is in your public schools. Those whose don't care to learn anything way outnumber those that do."

"The same for the secular church world. That includes millions upon millions of you who go to church. You worship your religious faith, instead of me, the Lord your God of heaven. As I said, I am not a religion! I am, Jesus Christ, who was, is, and is to come!"

"I am the Living One I was dead, and now look, I am alive for ever and ever. And I hold the keys of death and Hades." (Revelation 1:18 NIV)

"I am the Lord your God, manifested in the flesh among man. You ever read that about me? Probably not!"

"The Word became flesh and made his dwelling among us. We have seen his glory, the glory of the one and Only Son, who came from the Father, full of grace and truth." (John 1:14 NIV)

"So, what is allowed in your public schools shouldn't really matter in futuristic terms. Even if education of religions weren't allowed in your public schools, what are you teaching the children at home about me? All they see is you strung out on drugs! They see you drunk! They see you beating their mom! They see you nagging, and nagging, and complaining to their father over matters that don't make sense to them."

"They see you with another man or woman that is not their parent! They watch everything and anything on social media when you're not paying attention! Especially video games that are satanic in their own way."

"Need I go on? It really starts at home in what you plant in your children's heart. So instead of planting a future of fame and fortune, plant me in their heart," says the Lord! "For they will need me like you will in the days to come like you would've **NEVER** imagined."

"In case you haven't noticed, other legislation laws are wanting to be passed among you without you being aware of it."

"Like what Lord?"

"Do you know it has been brought up to pass a law that would require all the young children of your society to be chipped with a microchip, like they do animals!"

"What?"

"Yes. Plant chips in your children to help fight kidnappings, and child abductions that occur on a constant basis over parents fighting over custody of children in divorce cases; perverts and pedophiles kidnapping children to sexually molest them, or use them in sexual prostitution. Good intentions on the chipping, but bad motive!"

"Start looking around you! Employers are, or want to start, micro-chipping their employees! Considering the majority of you know that the chip is the number of a man that is mentioned by my apostle John in the book of Revelation. That is why it is written,

"He who has ears, let Him hear what the Spirit of God says."

(Revelation 2:29, 3:23)

"Do you not see that Satan is focused on your children, and your grandchildren? He could care less about you adults!"

"What? He's got every one of you where he wants you: angry at me over a situation that broke your heart; in rebellion towards me because you would rather live your perverted lives, than live for me, or in doubt of me, because you don't even believe I, the Lord God of heaven and earth, even exist."

"And you church goers can't even get along with one another because of all your names of religions, faiths and denominations. My Son cried and prayed for all of you to be **ONE!** So while all of you 'adults' are busy fighting amongst yourselves about what religion is right, and which one isn't, Satan is after your children and grandchildren while setting up his one world government system right underneath your noses, while you are so focused on leaving this world."

"But I say to you," says the Lord, "if you care to microchip anyone to keep up with them and their whereabouts, microchip the kidnappers, pedophiles, and parents who kidnap their own kids. Especially you snakes who have built a kingdom of human trafficking involving the very innocent lives of children. **LEAVE THE CHILDREN ALONE**," says the Lord!

"For it written unto all of you,

"If anyone causes one of these little ones – those who believe in me – to stumble it would be better for them to have a large millstone hung around their neck and to be drowned in the depths of the sea."

(Matthew 18:6 – Mark 9:42 – Luke 17:2 NIV)

That is why I demand every one of you to raise and train your children in the way they should go. The way being, Jesus Christ, my Son! Bring them to the foot of the cross after you first decide to go there yourself."

"This event of micro chipping people is already in your faces! I know you see it all over social media. But I know you have already come up with in your heart, and mental decision on thinking, taking the chip is different than taking the mark of the beast! The mark of the beast is 666! Glad you know that! But it is also the number of a man! All of you have a number known as a social security. So what are you doing?"

"Well, we are very excited that your return is very near Lord!"

"Every vision my Prophet, Daniel, had is leading to one final great

121

beast he sees appear on the earth. He is going to be far worse than any evil man who has appeared on this earth you live in. Yet he will have the look of a very deceptive good looking individual with good intentions. Sort of like the kings of past days you have honored and worshipped with your lives."

"Elvis, king of Rock and roll! Michael Jackson, king of pop! Jesus Christ, King of kings! What? Yes! That's how you honor my Son! Like one of your own! Yet he wasn't! Because he existed at one time, and now he doesn't!"

"**<u>YOU ARE A LIAR!</u>** He is my Son, the one TRUE King, and Lord of lords, who brought you peace, but not of this world! Yet you rejected Him! So this world ruler will use his greatest weapon against all *my people* which has been the biggest outcry of every living soul on the face of the earth: Peace! And who do you think that might be? Did you say the anti-christ? Guess what? You're right! The one <u>WHO WILL RULE </u>the entire world under his spell, and power of his own religion that will require you worshipping Him by chipping every one of you."

"But since you know so much about my word, you still won't totally repent of your ignorance in thinking you will be gone before he shows up. They only way you will be gone is if I call you home before then! Other than that, you will be here to see that coward. His appearing on this earth has nothing to do with my second coming! My second coming will be to put an end to his reign on earth, for torturing my people, along with his efforts of elevating Himself above me, the Lord God of Heaven and earth. This is exactly what you have been doing throughout the ages by judging and condemning *my people,* instead of loving them, and praying for them."

"Oh! And just because I require you to love everyone doesn't mean you have to go by, and agree with, what they feel, think, or what they want. My Son, Jesus Christ, was never persuaded to be like any of you. He just loved you, and forgave you, but never gave into you and your ways of rebellion, and selfish interest. And guess what, it cost Him his life!"

"So! Either you commit unto me with your whole heart, or keep being the hypocrite you are with one foot in heaven, and the other foot on earth. You choose this day whom you will serve: yourself or me, the Lord your God, who created you in my image. The judgments that are coming even before the anti-Christ shows up are the elements of the earth crying out to me, their creator. My Son, Jesus Christ's blood still cries out to me for what was done to Him then, and is being done unto Him now this very day. Vengeance is mine," says the Lord!

"I said **VENGEANCE!** Vengeance for my temple! Vengeance for my temple! The one who said to all of you:

"Destroy this temple, and I will raise it in three days."   (John 2:19 NIV)

"And that's exactly what all of you did. You destroyed Him, but three days later I rose Him back up! And, for what? To give you the healing and forgiveness of your sins, and peace into your lives you desired to have in me," says the Lord! "You accepted that with no problem into your lives by coming into the resurrected temple by way of the north gate, through your knowledge and reasoning within your own minds; also the east and west gates, my extended arms of love and forgiveness for you that you take for granted. Yet, you change not your heart towards me," says the Spirit of the Lord!

"And for doing so, you failed to receive the Promised Holy Spirit! That is why you non-followers of mine have conviction of sins in your life which allows you to believe in me, yet you do what you want. And you followers of mine, you judge and condemn everybody to hell with no conscience on your souls knowing that, **I WILL** that no one perishes."

"Therefore, I say to all of you, <u>I WILL TAKE VENGEANCE FOR</u>

MY TEMPLE! I will exact vengeance for my temple, unless you come to the foot of the cross where you will find deliverance for your souls. The temple inside of you resists my resurrected Christ and his glorious power into his proper place of residing within your heart, soul and spirit. I do not dwell in temples built by man! Don't you remember being told that and asked?"

"This is what the Lord says: Heaven is my throne, and the earth is my footstool. Where is the house you will build for me? Where will my resting place be?"
(Isaiah 66:1, Acts 7:49 NIV)

"I speak not of churches you consider temples, but your souls within you, which are not temples built by man. Yes, I created you for my purpose which is yet to be fulfilled in your life. Why? Because you came from man! You remember the teaching I gave of being born again? Probably not!"

"In reply Jesus declared, I tell you the truth, no one can see the kingdom of God unless he is born again. How can a man be born again when he is old? Nicodemus asked. Surely he cannot enter a second time into his mother's womb to be born! Jesus answered, I tell you the truth, NO ONE can enter the kingdom of God unless he is born of water and the Spirit. Flesh gives birth to flesh, but the Spirit gives birth to spirit. You should not be surprised at my saying, you must be born again."
(John 3:3-7 NIV)

"Flesh gave birth to flesh when you came into the world. But in order for you to return to God, your creator, you must be born again of water and the Spirit. Why? Because you were born into the realm of sin that covers the earth like a veil covers a woman's face. You can see through the veil, but not in its fullness and clarity. That is why you are stuck on trying to figure out who your mother or father really is, or why wasn't I wanted by them?"

"What if I, the Lord your God, told you, I personally allowed you to be born, but for **ONE** purpose: to be my son or my daughter who will live with me forever and ever in my eternal kingdom! I am trying to remove that veil of confusion, religions, faiths and denominations off your faces, and more importantly, your self-wills! And it can be done only if you are born again of water and the Spirit."

"That is why I am trying to get you to come unto me through the south gate of the temple, through the foot of the cross! Where the water that came from heaven can clear your eyesight in seeing the truth that will set you free in the prison of the world you live in."

"All of you get water baptized at one point in your life, or another. Right? Most of you? That is used as the symbol of the water I spoke of in being born again, ceremonial water baptisms through the church? That was what John the Baptist did for the people in his days here on earth, except he was in a river, not a church! He said:

"I baptize you with water for repentance. But after me will come one who is more powerful than I, whose sandals I am not fit to carry. He will baptize you with the Holy Spirit and with fire." (Matthew 3:11 NIV)

"Which apparently meant there was more to giving of yourself to me other than just through water baptism. That is why you have millions of followers of religion who get water baptized and the only thing that changes in their life on that day of baptism is their hairdo and their clothes that got wet that day. Oh, and their beautiful makeup they spent hours preparing themselves with to look pretty got washed off, or messed up. Other than that, nothing changed in their hearts towards me and their lives."

"Come to the foot of the cross of the resurrected temple with a sincere heart of repentance and see if your life doesn't change. It is the place where the water and blood flowed in a downward motion onto you, courtesy of the Love Christ Jesus, my Son, has for you who was pierced and wounded for your transgressions."

"Now it was the day of preparation, and the next day was to be a special Sabbath. Because the Jews did not want the bodies left on the crosses during the

Sabbath, they asked Pilate to have the legs broken and the bodies take down. The soldiers therefore came and broke the legs of the first man who had been crucified with Jesus, and then those of the other. But when they came to Jesus and found that he was already dead, they did not break his legs. Instead, one of the soldiers pierced Jesus' side with a spear, bringing a sudden flow of blood and water."

(John 19:31-34 NIV)

"But he was pierced for our transgressions, he was crushed for our iniquities; the punishment that brought us peace was upon Him, and by his wounds we are healed."   *(Isaiah 53:5NIV)*

"Do you see now, why I want you to come to the foot of the cross, the south gate of the temple? I am about to take vengeance for my temple that was destroyed, and ignored even after I resurrected it in three days!"

"These things happened so that the scriptures would be fulfilled: Not one of his bones will be broken, and, as another scripture says, They will look on the one they have pierced."   *(John 19:36 NIV)*

"When you come to the foot of the cross, you have no choice but to look up…to my Son's suffering and sacrifice he gave unto you for your life, instead of looking down on Him and everybody else in and around your life through his crowned pierced head and loving opened arms of love. At his feet you will have no choice but to look up from the ground and cry as you look unto the one you have pierced. That was why you were told, 'Look up your redemption draws near!'"

"When these things begin to take place, stand up and lift your heads, because your redemption is drawing near."   *(Luke 21:28 NIV)*

"And there is only way **ONE** place you can be in in order to look up while lifting your head: at the foot of the cross!"

"Who is it that overcomes the world? <u>ONLY</u> the one who believes that Jesus is

the Son of God. This is the one who came by water and blood – Jesus Christ. He did not come by water only, but by water and blood. And it is the Spirit who testifies, because the Spirit is truth. For there are three that testify: the Spirit, the water and the blood; and the three are in agreement. We accept human testimony, but God's testimony is greater because it is the testimony of God, which he has given about his Son. Whoever believes in the Son of God accepts this testimony. Whoever does not believe, God has made Him out to be a liar, because they have not believed the testimony God has given about his Son. And this is the testimony: God has given us eternal life, and this life is in his Son. Whoever has the Son has life, whoever does not have the Son of God does not have life."

(1 John 5:5-12 NIV)

'For in the time of the end it is written:

"Look, he is coming with the clouds, <u>AND EVERY EYE WILL SEE HIM</u>, even those who pierced Him; all the peoples of the earth will mourn because of Him. So shall it be! Amen. I am the Alpha and the Omega, says the Lord God, who is, and who was, and who is to come, the Almighty."

(Revelation 1:7-8 NIV)

"Look, I am coming soon! My reward is with me, and I will give to each person according to what they have done." *(Revelation 22:12 NIV)*

"You can stress yourself out if you want to by looking over your whole life and wonder what all you have done wrong, or right. But unlike the people you live among, I do not look at what you are doing in your life, or what you have done in your life. I am watching over every one of you in what you have done, or are doing with my Son that I gave you from my very loving and forgiving heart," says the Lord! "I am about to take vengeance for my temple," says the Lord. "**<u>NOT YOUR LIVES!</u>** So I say to you:

"If my people, who are called by my name, will humble themselves and pray and seek my face and turn from their wicked ways, then I will hear from heaven, and I will forgive their sin and will heal their land." *(2 Chronicles 7:14 NIV)*

"My people? Yes! You, my chosen one!"

"Then he said: The God of our ancestors has chosen you to know his will and to see the Righteous One (Jesus Christ) *and to hear words from his mouth."*

(Acts 22:14 NIV)

"Called by My Name? Yes, the name of Jesus Christ! The living temple! That is the only name I am calling you by!"

"For there is one God and one mediator between God and mankind, the man Christ Jesus." *(1 Timothy 2:5 NIV)*

"Pray and seek my Face? Yes, my face!"

*"For God, who said, Let light shine out of darkness, made his light shine in our hearts to give us the light of the knowledge of God's glory displayed in the **FACE** of Christ."* *(2 Corinthians 4:6 NIV)*

"Turn from your wicked ways? Yes your wicked ways of totally ignoring my Son, Jesus Christ, as your Lord and Savior! That is far worse than any sin you have ever committed in the life you have lived. He came to forgive you of your sins, yet you take his death for granted as a free token into heaven, or just totally ignore it. That was why it is written about my Son, Jesus Christ,

"Whoever believes in Him is not condemned, but whoever does not believe stands condemned already because they have not believed in the name of God's one and only Son." *(John 3:18 NIV)*

*"Be on your guard; stand firm in the faith, be courageous, be strong. **Do EVERYTHING in LOVE**."* *(1 Corinthians 16:13-14 NIV)*

"Believe in my Son, Jesus Christ, that I may heal your lives and forgive you from your blindness of religions that you listen to that never give you freedom from your sins," says the Lord!

"If anyone does not Love the Lord, let that person be cursed! Come, Lord! The grace of the Lord Jesus be with you. My Love to all of you in Christ Jesus name. Amen." *(1 Corinthians 16:22-24 NIV)*

ENEMIES OF THE CROSS

*"He who testifies to these things says, 'Yes, I Am coming soon.' Amen, Come, Lord Jesus. The grace of the Lord Jesus be with **God's** people. Amen!"*

(Revelation 22:20-21 NIV)

129

ABOUT THE AUTHOR

Javier Macias says, "I stand on the authority of the word of God that enables me to see beyond what is seen with the naked eye. Our future is now, Jesus Christ!"

Javier's personal task, and calling, is, "Jesus Christ, and none other!"
He receives messages from God in very unique ways. They can come through a movie, a conversation being carried on by others, a simple gesture made by someone, or a spoken word directly to him from God Himself.

Javier says, "As a servant and Prophet of the Lord, I will not be held accountable unto the Lord for anyone's blood! When called upon to do a work, it must be done with reverence towards the One who called one to do it."

Javier Macias is the founder of, "We Rock Youth Ministries!" We Rock Youth Ministries! is a non-profit, 501(c3) status organization, incorporated in 1999.

We Rock Youth Ministry's foundational faith statement is:

"Therefore if you have any encouragement from being united with Christ, if any comfort from his Love, if any common sharing in the Spirit, if any tenderness and compassion, then make my joy complete by being like-minded, having the same Love, being in one Spirit and of one mind.

Do nothing out of selfish ambition or vain conceit. Rather in humility value others above yourselves, not looking to your own interests but each of you to the interest of others. In your relationships with one another, have the SAME MINDSET as Christ Jesus: Who being in very nature God did not consider equality with God something to be used to his own advantage; rather, he made himself nothing by taking the very nature of a servant being made in human likeness. And being found in appearance as a man, he humbled himself by becoming obedient to death- even death on the cross! Therefore God exalted him to the highest place and gave him the name that is above every name, that at the name of Jesus every knee should bow, in heaven and on the earth and under the earth, and EVERY tongue acknowledge that Jesus Christ is Lord, to the glory of God the Father." (Philippians 2:1-11, NIV)

"Look, he is coming with the clouds," and "every eye will see him, even those who pierced him"; and all peoples on earth "will mourn because of him." So shall it be! Amen.

"I AM the Alpha and the Omega," says the Lord God, "who is, and who was, and who is to come, the Almighty."

(Revelation 1:7-8 NIV)

"The word of the Lord came to me, saying, 'Before I formed you in the womb I knew you, before you were born I set you apart; I appointed you as a prophet to the nations.'" (Jeremiah 1:4-5)

"You must speak my words to them, whether they listen or fail to listen, for they are rebellious. But you, son of man, listen to what I say to you. Do not rebel like that rebellious people; open your mouth and eat what I give you." Then I looked, and I saw a hand stretched out to me. In it was a scroll, which he unrolled before me. On both sides of it were written words of lament and mourning and woe." (Ezekiel 2:7-10)

"Son of man, I have made you a watchman for the people of Israel; so hear the word I speak and give them warning from me." (Ezekiel 33:7)

"But if the watchman sees the sword coming and does not blow the trumpet to warn the people and the sword comes and takes someone's life, that persons life will be taken because of their sin, but I will hold the watchman accountable for their blood."   (Ezekiel 33:6)

"Say to them, 'As surely as I live,' declares the Sovereign Lord, 'I take no pleasure in the death of the wicked, but rather that they turn from their ways and live. Turn! Turn from your evil ways! Why will you die, people of Israel?'"   (Ezekiel 33:11)

"At this I fell at his feet to worship him. But he said to me, 'Do not do it! I AM a fellow servant with you and with your brothers who hold to the testimony of Jesus. Worship God! For the testimony of Jesus is the Spirit of prophecy.'"   (Revelation 19:10)

Sincerely, in Jesus Christ's Love!
Prophet Javier Macias